:

p

Anger Control Parenting

To order additional copies, please contact us.
BookSurge, LLC
www.booksurge.com
1-866-308-6235
orders@booksurge.com

Anger Control Parenting

How to Effectively Discipline Your
Children with Confidence
and Self-Control

Vivian Lamphear, Ph.D.
And
Sherry Marlar

Foreword by
Stephen Arterburn, M.Ed.
Founder of New Life Ministries
and Radio Host of New Life Live

2006

Anger Control Parenting

TABLE OF CONTENTS

I lovingly dedicate this book to the mothers and women I meet on my humanitarian trips to Africa and Haiti. From their meager resources and at great personal sacrifice, they selflessly start orphanages for the children of AIDS. Inspired by these caring women, I am donating all of my proceeds from Anger Control Parenting products to their efforts through the organization, Save Africa's Children (www.saveafricaschildren.org).
Vivian Shaw Lamphear

ACKNOWLEDGEMENTS

This book is the culmination of my personal and professional journey to understand the mechanics of aggressive and chaotic family systems and to teach effective ways to prevent their development and escalation.

My mother inspired this book. Overcoming incredible adversity and raising six children on her own, she modeled strength and forbearance. For what they give up so I can help others, I give my love and gratitude to my husband Ken, my daughter Ryan Michelle, and my son Dylan. Together we celebrate the creation of a healthy, happy family system. This book is also for our children's children who will continue a new lineage of loving, Christian families.

I thank Reverend Harold and Shirley Korver, who have shown us, by example, how to love our children and remain committed to God, marriage and family. Reverend Ken and Lisa Korver, Bishop and Mrs. Charles Blake, and Missionary Eleanor Workman, thank you for modeling the importance of living beyond ourselves, and loving and serving others, to the glory of God.

My sister and surrogate mother, Cyndy Jaeger, R.N., provided me with love and support on this and other writing projects. I give a special thank you for her extensive editing of an earlier version of Anger Control Parenting. As a parent of twins, her feedback and suggestions were invaluable. Sandra Sudjian also made important contributions to an earlier version of Anger Control Parenting. Her Master's thesis demonstrates and discusses the effectiveness of the Anger Control Parenting Program. Also, a debt of gratitude is owed to James Marlar for his continued support and essential computer expertise, and the countless hours he contributed to the final preparation process.

I express heartfelt gratitude to Dr. G. R. Patterson for his support and encouragement at various phases of my clinical career. His seminal work revealed how and why violent family systems develop, and he provided a direction for hope and change. I am also indebted to Drs. Raymond Novaco, Constance Hanf, Rex Forehand, Sheila Eyberg, and many others whose clinical research in anger, parent-child interactions, and parenting interventions are reflected in these pages. Drs. Forehand & McMahon's book, The Noncompliant Child, is referenced extensively in this book with permission from Guilford Press and provides the basis for many of the behavioral change concepts. Dr. Novaco's seminal anger research and anger model are referenced in the discussion of anger.

And, to those who have lived through family aggression and chaos, who desperately want to build new, healthier family systems based on mutual love and respect, I want to share this book and the hope and knowledge that:

All things are possible through God who strengthens us.

V.S.L.

FOREWORD

When Dr. Lamphear asked me to review her *Anger Control Parenting* book, I was already familiar with some of her work in the field of clinical psychology. She has spent over 25 years researching, developing, and providing better ways of strengthening families. We have worked together on prior projects including co-authoring the *Gentle Eating* book and the *Gentle Eating Workbook*. I readily agreed to her request.

The main focus of Dr. Lamphear's *Anger Control Parenting* book and seminars is to teach parents how to control their anger while they effectively discipline their children. Through my work as Founder and Chairman of New Life Ministries, I am well aware of how parent-child interactions can escalate out of control. Anger is a common denominator in many of these negative family patterns.

The high levels of stress many families experience today underscore the need for effective strategies that parents can rely on. *Anger Control Parenting* provides much needed child management and anger control techniques for parents, caregivers and teachers in their quest to raise emotionally healthy, morally responsible children. This book will benefit all who read, study, and put into practice what they have learned.

STEPHEN ARTERBURN, M.Ed.
Founder and Chairman,
New Life Ministries

PREFACE

Fantasizing about what it would be like to have children, many of us imagined how we would love and nurture our young ones. We dreamed about the fun we'd have spending time with them and teaching them new things. For many parents, such tender moments are few and far between compared to the sometimes overwhelming challenge of child-raising. There are many times when our children's prolonged bouts of whining and bickering are enough to put us over the edge. This is especially true when we're tired or under extra stress. We get into parent-child debates, often reacting angrily and indignantly, and the seemingly endless barrage of confrontations leaves us emotionally and mentally battered and bruised.

Until recently, the reality of parenting (with which both authors have had firsthand experience!) seldom was shared openly. Parents are reluctant to admit they have difficulty controlling their anger when they discipline. Many parents report feeling they are the only ones struggling to get their children to obey. To admit limitations seems tantamount to validating their deepest fear: That perhaps they are not cut out to be good parents. This Anger Control Parenting (ACP) book directly addresses and explores these realities and fears. Like most of you, both authors have been in the trenches of parenthood. Using the skills outlined in the ACP program made the experience easier and more enjoyable.

Probably, all of us have engaged in and witnessed incidents ruled by angry outbursts. *Anger is a wind that blows out the lamp of the mind* is a poetic definition and one that leaps to the heart of the anger matter in few words. But, realizing what anger *is* and *being prepared to control and defuse that powerful emotion* are two different things. Easy to implement strategies and solutions for anger management are outlined and discussed in this book.

Under the best circumstances young children can be extremely frustrating. They usually think and move slower and struggle for words to express themselves. In contrast, situations involving children escalate quickly and change rapidly. Often, parents fail to evaluate their actions and reactions, and the actions and reactions of their children. Nevertheless, parents must learn to "Stop, Look, and Listen" before leaping into heated verbal exchanges that may lead to emotional and physical abuse. *Avoid letting push come to shove.*

Children strive to do the forbidden just one more time and do not like delay in gratification. They whine and scream in protest when they are told "No." Although teenagers are similar to adults in many of their capabilities, our limit setting often seems illogical to them and their protests seem endless to us.

Parents must take responsibility for what they have or have not taught their children. Our tendency as parents is to blame our children for their behavior. "Bailey never listens." "Zach can't keep things in order." "Hayden rarely comes when I call him." "Jacqui constantly argues about curfews and chore assignments." The fact is: Our children behave according to the consequences *we* provide. *In essence, our children are who we make them.*

When you cannot get your children to obey, you experience intense frustration because you do not understand why your efforts are failing. ACP will teach you why your discipline efforts have failed and what you need to do to have well-behaved, respectful kids. As you read, learn, practice and implement the procedures outlined, you will understand clearly what mistakes you've made: You will learn effective discipline measures and how to control your anger toward your children.

CHAPTER 1

"ONCE UPON A TIME . . ."

INTRODUCTION TO ANGER CONTROL PARENTING

" . . . **not so very long ago,**" many parents may have felt they were in a leaky boat traveling in turbulent waters surrounded by their disobedient children, while other parents were sailing on smooth waters with their well-behaved children in tow. That fairytale mindset has been dispelled: Now, parents are sharing stories of their family struggles with a goal of patching the boat and calming the waters. They are worn out from expending their energies without achieving positive results, and are searching for help from a proven source.

Anger Control Parenting (ACP) is a clinically proven parenting book providing that source. *ACP teaches scientifically based methods of both anger control and child management*, and gives you a clear understanding of why your children behave as they do. ACP will:

- Teach you how to make positive changes in your behavior and your children's behavior.
- Show you that controlling your anger while you discipline builds and preserves closeness with your children and keeps their self-esteem intact.
- Teach you to anticipate future parent-child problems and how to prevent or solve such problems.

Our desire in parenting is to raise psychologically secure and morally responsible children. Though love and affection are essential parenting nutrients, *they are not enough*. Parents also must develop effective discipline measures and put into practice pre-determined consequences for their children's negative behavior. Providing consistent consequences following your children's behavior requires that *you* have an abundance of self-discipline. Consistency is critical and becomes more automatic as you work through the ACP training.

Dr. T. Berry Brazelton, a clinical professor of pediatrics emeritus at Harvard Medical School, has been a pediatrician for more than 50 years. He is considered by many to be the pre-eminent name in child rearing in this country today. When queried about how problems differed now from his early days of practice, Dr. Brazelton responded (Reprint Courtesy of the Fort Worth Star-Telegram):

> *. . . One of the things that's gotten away from us these days is discipline, building in teaching about how to control yourself, how to stop yourself. . . . Discipline is one of the things that's gone way down for this generation.*

Instead of a hodgepodge of techniques, ACP is a conceptually integrated approach allowing you to develop new tactics as future problem behaviors arise. Each chapter helps you to learn and remember important concepts and skills. If you make a strong commitment to understanding, practicing, and implementing the methods outlined in each chapter, you will notice positive changes in your behavior and your child's behavior. As you model more loving and respectful ways of interacting, your family will experience a more cooperative and loving atmosphere.

ACP recognizes that anger control is an essential parenting skill and addresses the importance of this vital element in a parent-child relationship. In fact, setting forth the value, merits, and results of anger control, and outlining anger control skills, is the most unique aspect of ACP.

Parents often come to my seminars hoping to learn new ways to punish their kids to get them to obey. As you will soon learn, *punishment alone does not achieve lasting behavior change and tends to damage the parent-child relationship.* For that reason, ACP relies on what behavioral research shows works best: That initially using the most positive means of discipline is preferable because it is more effective and has less negative "side effects." In ACP, parents are *first* trained to change their children's behavior with *positive methods only.* Then, if needed, positive methods are combined with more punishing methods. Some children respond almost exclusively to positive discipline methods. Other kids require the addition of more punishing methods.

Research shows that over time parents may remember to use the punishing methods, but positive praise and attention toward their child dwindles. ACP emphasizes teaching parents *first* how to notice and praise their child's positive behaviors. **Result:** Positive child behaviors increase and the parent-child relationship becomes closer and more loving. Next, parents continue using the positive methods as they learn how to respond to their child's lingering negative behaviors in a calm, matter-of-fact manner by providing consequences that have meaning to the child. **Result:** Negative behaviors decrease and children become more respectful and obedient.

GETTING THE MOST BENEFIT FROM ACP

In each chapter, child management *and* anger control materials are discussed. Using guidelines provided, parents may continue practicing skills and implementing new procedures. Throughout the program, illustrations pull the whole program together.

Listening to the ACP relaxation compact discs (CDs) and practicing the anger control skills outlined in this book will help you to work through challenging situations. You will:

- Learn to demonstrate self-control while you effectively discipline your child.
- Learn methods to control your anger and get the results you want by viewing the interaction as a detached third party.
- Learn that remaining calm and not getting drawn into battle allows for clear thinking and effective problem solving.

Implementing the scientifically proven methods given requires a commitment of time as well as energy. Though desired changes may appear to evolve slowly in some instances, consistency and follow-through assure positive results. **A major reward for staying the course with the ACP techniques is witnessing how your discipline efforts are transformed into self-discipline in your child.**

ACP: Built On a Firm Foundation

The research and theoretical basis of Anger Control Parenting is derived from the seminal work of Hanf (1969), Patterson (1976), Forehand & McMahon (1981), and Novaco (1976). These researchers have shown:

- Parents and children influence each other's behavior,
- the influence is bi-directional and reciprocal, and
- changes in the behavior of one person impacts the behavior of others.

Based on behavioral principles of reward and punishment, this is called the **social learning approach**. Social learning principles taught in this book are the basic building blocks of effective child discipline.

Most parenting books focus on teaching parents how to change their children's *negative* behavior. ACP follows the reciprocal view of child management: Parents influence children's behavior and children influence the behavior of their parents. For example: A child's dawdling can frustrate parents inciting them to feel angry and yell, "I said, get dressed now! Can't you ever listen?"

You will learn how such *negative attention* increases your child's dawdling. Further, a constant stream of angry comments flowing from parent to child can impair the child's self-esteem.

A familiar example of social learning:

- Kaily asks to watch TV; Mom answers, "No."
- Kaily whines and yells; Mom gives in reluctantly and says, "Okay, but just 20 minutes."

Mom has just reinforced Kaily's persistence in whining and disrespectful yelling. The next time Mom says "No," Kaily is more likely to protest because it previously worked and Mom gave in. When Kaily whines and yells, Mom is more likely to give in because that response stopped Kaily's *torturous* whining! In this example, both Mom and Kaily negatively influenced each other's behavior. Mom needs to learn how to teach Kaily that "No" is "No" and disrespectful responses will not be tolerated. You will learn more about negative reinforcement in Chapter 4.

Dr. G.R. Patterson, through clinical studies, found that parents often rely on *coercive strategies* (yelling, physical punishment) to get their kids to obey. These *reflexive* strategies work initially and the child obeys. However, as children get used to their parent's yelling and spanking, these coercive strategies are less effective. When obedience decreases, parents *escalate* their negative coercive behavior, putting the child at risk for emotional and physical harm. Under the *coercion theory*, parents escalate their verbal and physical aggression as a last resort to make their children obey. ***When other means fail, we get angry.***

In fact, results of a recent study of almost 1,000 families yielded these disturbing findings:

- 75% of parents participating in the study admitted to angrily yelling at their kids.

- Angry yelling and shouting at children in an effort to modify negative behavior is considered *psychological aggression* and can adversely affect children's self-esteem.

Results of a scientific study of ACP are very encouraging. After only eight weeks of ACP training, parents reported significant decreases in their anger and in their children's problem behaviors (Sudjian & Lamphear, 1995).

FAMILY GOALS — A Framework for Happier Households

As you prepare to set sail on a new parenting course, it is an ideal time to consider what *goals* you have for your family. You might reflect on the type of *family environment* you desire to create: Perhaps a warm, encouraging family with more relaxed down time, parents yelling less, kids obeying the first time, etc. This will involve changing not only your and your children's behaviors, but your family's behaviors and priorities as well. You might call a family meeting (see below) to discuss behavioral goals for individual family members and the family as a whole. Emphasize that *with cooperation the goals can be attained.*

Families might also discuss the overall focus and purpose of their family in the larger community and world. Do we constantly compete to get ahead materially only to keep the fruits of our labor all to ourselves? Or do we view our family as playing a vital role in making the world a better place by sharing our blessings and talents with others? Keep in mind that children will model what we *do*, not what we *say* they should do.

Listed are examples of family goals:

1. Creating a safe haven where every family member is nurtured and encouraged.

2. Learning to resolve conflicts without verbal or physical hurts and abuses.

3. Creating a home where there are no ongoing failures and setbacks are used as lessons for learning; and no family member is made to feel inferior in any way.

4. Letting each family member know they are loved and respected for who they are, and valued for their uniqueness.
5. Planning mealtimes that include all family members (when possible).
6. Setting aside time for family activities.
7. Expecting children to follow rules parents set in place; parents willing to follow-through with necessary consequences if rules are broken.
8. Building a strong spiritual base for the family.
9. Learning to show feelings of love and fondness for each other.
10. Periodically collecting and distributing food and clothing (or other necessities) to aid the less fortunate.

DROPPING ANCHOR AND GATHERING 'ROUND — Family Meetings

Family meetings provide a forum for your kids to give updates on their activities. Discussions can focus on home life, outlining good things already in place and, if appropriate, exploring ways to make changes to benefit family harmony. Thoughts might also be voiced about relationships between family members, where to go on vacations, or how chores should be allocated. Give each person a turn speaking. In discussing what behavior changes could be made, avoid attacking family members directly.

Ask for and validate your kids' opinions; let them know you will think about what they have said. It is important for one of the parents to summarize the discussions and to clarify points, if necessary. Parents are encouraged to seek their children's opinions on various topics, and to aid them in reasoning through a question or problem. This builds excellent problem solving skills.

Ideally, weekly family meetings would become a tradition for your family:

*   Family meetings aid development of a greater sense of family identity, cohesion, and closeness. Values and expected behavior in your family can be clarified.
*   Family meetings provide a forum for negotiation and for teaching and modeling conflict resolution.

- Family meetings allow for discussion of progress on behavior changes and what needs to happen next.

Turning That Frown Upside Down! Use a fun theme for a meeting of family members. Announce family plans to turn frowns *upside down*, and emphasize that *a frown is just a smile waiting to happen!* You might display a smiley-face and turn it upside down to show that the smile becomes a frown and vice versa as the face is rotated. Let the children know that attitudes, moods, and behaviors can be changed — or, *rotated* — to *do away with a frown* and *make a smile happen!*

The children might be told:

"We are making some changes so that the family gets along better. We want to have more family fun times and not fight and argue so much. Each of us needs to work harder to show more love and kindness. We want to have a happier family and home-life. When we ask you to do something, we expect you to obey promptly. For now, we will keep track of how well you obey by marking on a chart that has your name on it. We will do other things later. Mom and Dad will work on yelling less, talking nicer to everyone, and not being so grouchy. So, all of us will make changes so our home is a happier place."

It is helpful if parents understand that: **The possession and use of power permeates every aspect of the human experience.** In most relationship situations — including parent-child relationships — the overarching dynamic is negotiation of power. **Parents must make it clear to their children that parental authority (or, power) is not negotiable.** Of course, children's thoughts and feelings will be elicited and considered. Ultimately, however, it is the parents who will make the final decisions as to what is best for their children and the family.

Parents who exhibit self-confidence in interactions with their children usually maintain more control, and their children feel more secure and are often more respectful. Your feelings and attitudes regarding *your* self-worth constantly affect your self-confidence. Therefore, study, think, grow — hone your parental skills. Act with love and kindness and become the most effective parent you can be!

PULLING UP ANCHOR — Setting a Course for Change

Discuss the changes you desire to make with all family members and get them onboard! For example, you might say:

"We are going to make some changes in our family. Mom and Dad need to do a better job teaching you certain behaviors. So, now we are going to try something new. In order for you to do the things you like to do, such as watch TV, play with friends, go to the mall, and do other things, we expect you to behave in a certain way. We expect you to do what we ask, talk with respect, keep your rooms clean, do other chores, and do your homework. We have listed the behaviors we expect. The chart shows the number of times you need to exhibit the behaviors each morning and night to earn certain privileges. Mom and Dad are going to work on being less grouchy." (You can use this dialogue when you begin the chart phase of ACP).

The following dialogue may be useful in discussing family changes with younger children:

Parent: "Colleen, there are things you do and ways that you behave that Mommy and Daddy are glad about. You almost always come when we call and you get yourself ready nicely for school. But, somehow we haven't taught you not to whine when we tell you 'No' about something or ask you to do a chore. We have a new plan to help you to learn how to express your anger by speaking clearly without whining.

"Each time we say, 'No' and you don't whine, you get a point, like this (demonstrate with the chart). But when you forget and whine, we will mark a negative point, like this (demonstrate). In order for you to talk on the 'phone, be with your friends, and watch TV, or play with special toys, you need to earn 10 total points before school (6:30 to 7:30 a.m.) and 10 points after school (3 to 5 p.m.). (Total negative points minus total points = Grand Total.) You've learned a lot of behaviors we like and we know you can learn not to whine, too!"

Notice two main points:

- **First**, behavior is discussed as something that is learned and can be changed. Whining is not considered a trait the child is born with; rather it is a behavior that developed because the parents did not teach the child how to behave otherwise.
- **Second**, sincere encouragement is provided to the child, communicating that the parents believe in the child's ability to make the expected changes.

As with Child-Centered Play, discussed in Chapter 6, if the above dialogue does not feel natural to you, you may have to play-act how you say this at first. Stay with it! Despite possible negative, resistant reactions from family members, you are taking slow but steady steps toward lasting change.

Do not expect your children to totally embrace the program at first. To enlist their cooperation, it is often helpful to ask for their ideas and feelings regarding the program and specific points and rewards to be earned or removed. If allowed to make suggestions, children may cooperate more fully. Ultimately, however, let the children know that: *Parents will make the final decision as to what takes place.*

Resolving Issues From The Inside-Out

Learn to recognize and resolve issues that rob you of your self-confidence:

STOP!	Think. Pinpoint the issues.
LOOK!	Mentally, search for ways to resolve the issues.
LISTEN!	Reflect on memory-stored positive *coping statements* . Play the ACP relaxation compact discs (CDs).

Gather strength. Then, take action to: **Stop doctoring the symptoms! Cure the cause!**

AWARENESS FLASH! — Anger Never Travels Alone

The key to controlling and defusing anger is by understanding that: Anger never travels alone. It always has at least one traveling companion. When you feel anger welling up, learn to recognize these piggy-back emotions (among others):

- Extreme Stress
- Low Self-Worth
- Feeling Unappreciated
- Being Ignored
- Feeling Hopeless
- Feeling Powerless

- Sadness
- Defiance
- Guilt
- Feeling Disrespected
- Feeling Overwhelmed
- Alienation

These emotions will never be conquered; there are too many changing and shifting circumstances that affect every area of your life daily to hope for that. *What you can do to avoid losing your temper is:*

- Manage discipline problems and stressful incidents as they occur.
- Do not allow a buildup of frustration and helplessness to overwhelm you.
- Douse the hot spots before they flame.
- Act quickly to find solutions and deprive anger of the traveling companions it must have to gain motion.

It is difficult to stay calm, matter-of-fact, and consistent while your kids are screaming, talking back, or making disrespectful faces. *Though the temptation to take the path of least resistance is beckoning to you at every turn, it is not in the best interest of the children to take that route.* And, remember:

Rising tempers will not improve the immediate situation for parent or child.

A particular behavior children exhibit that sends parents' anger sparks flying is: When their children challenge or defy parental authority. But a wise parent understands the need for parents to model anger control for their children: Lead by example. Learn to detect your anger signs which may include:

- Pursed lips.
- Elevated heart rhythms.
- Rapid negative self-talk.
- A constriction of throat muscles.

- A feeling of tightening in your chest.
- Red splotches on your skin.
- Narrowed eyes

Then, take time to:

STOP!   Determine your child's intention.
LOOK!   View the situation from an impersonal standpoint.
           Is your child being defiant or just focused on wanting
           a toy, a treat, or more play-time?
LISTEN!   Is your child challenging your authority, or "pleading
           his case?"

After consideration, make appropriate decisions in a calm manner.

BANISH ANGER INDUCING "CULPRITS"

STOP!   The situation is racing out of control.
LOOK!   See the angry faces.
LISTEN!   Hear the angry words.

Take a moment to relax. Breathe deeply. Visualize an open trash basket. Now, toss the words **"Always"** and **"Never"** into the basket and close the lid.

Immediately, there is a calmer atmosphere because two anger inducing "culprits" have been banished!

Examples:

Toss:	"You're **always** so selfish. You **never** share."
Replace With:	"Sometimes you are selfish. You must learn to share."
Toss:	"You **always** want your way. You **never** consider others."
Replace With:	"You can't have your way every time. You need to learn to compromise."
Toss:	"You're **always** late, and **never** complete your chores on time."
Replace With:	"If you need to, start your chores earlier so you can complete them on time."
Toss:	"You **always** leave your clothes and toys scattered. You **never** pick up your things."
Replace With:	"Please pick up your clothes before playtime and put your toys away before bedtime."
Toss:	"You **always** embarrass me. You **never** allow me a minute for myself. You **never** mind. You **always** make things worse. You **never** listen."
Replace With:	"I know you can act nicely. Mommy is expecting company and I need you to help by playing with your little brother and sharing your toys. I will be close by if you need me. When I talk with you, please listen. If you don't understand what Mommy wants you to do, let me know and I will tell you again."

Beware of Loud, Louder, LOUDEST!

When family pressures stack up — unresolved — symptoms are shown in various ways by family members, who may:
- Retreat into silence.
- Become sarcastic or overly critical.
- Overreact to mundane incidents.
- Yell and shout with little provocation.
- Avoid other family members.

Children witnessing these behaviors are apt to mimic them. Do not get drawn into a yell-fest with your children: You get loud, they get louder; you get even louder, and they get louder still. **Understand that angry, sullen silence — either yours or theirs — will always be "loudest."**

Some childcare experts suggest that parents speak in a softer tone and lower their voices when disciplining children. This tactic often results in the children quieting to hear what is said. At the very least, the parents are exhibiting restraint and can view the incident more calmly without added drama. This is the emotional equivalent to advice penned by ancient philosopher Marcus Aurelius: *"Walk around the briar patch."*

A better example:

> *A soft answer turns away wrath, But a harsh word stirs up anger. Proverbs 15:1*

Always be aware of your words and actions:

- A young one's ears are always listening.
- A young one's eyes are always watching.
- A young one's mind is always remembering.

And, your body language can *speak* volumes: Refrain from using impatient, defensive gestures such as negative head-shaking, finger pointing, hands on hips, toe-tapping, or arms crossed on chest. Avoid displaying angry facial expressions which can be upsetting to your children and can inhibit your calming techniques.

"STICKS AND STONES . . ." — Pressures and Hurts Kids Experience

Most of us are familiar with the sing-song rhyme scheme of: *"Sticks and stones may break my bones, but words can never hurt me."* The reality is that words can — and do — hurt us. In a short timeframe, we could reel off any number of instances where thoughtless, hurtful remarks have been directed toward us or we have directed such remarks toward others. At times, our stress outbursts are hurled at family members — often our children — because they are "within shouting distance." Even as we seek to reduce *our* stress levels, we face another urgent consideration:

Do we fail to take note of the pressures our children face,

whether those pressures originate at home, in school, or other places outside the home? Just as we have meltdowns due to negative situations, so do our children. And, their behavioral patterns are also influenced by daily happenings which may cause them stress and hurt feelings.

Your children may not seek your help or advice if they are experiencing unpleasant verbal exchanges with playmates or classmates. Children usually find a way to level the playing field and are adept at delivering verbal slings and arrows: If they are displeased or upset with their peers they might say to them, "I won't invite you to my birthday party." Or, "You can't sit with me at lunchtime." Or, perhaps, they rely on *name dropping*: "I don't like you and Robin doesn't like you either." However, if you notice that your child exhibits continued anger and aggression and has become disruptive or unreasonable, there may be a deeper concern that needs to be addressed: Mocking and teasing by peers.

A common practice among some groups is to mock and tease "outsiders" about their weight, hairstyle, choice of clothing, grades, height, manner of speaking, or anything that will generate reactions the ones taunting find amusing. Mocking and teasing among elementary students often morph into bullying as students enter middle school. In fact (Reprint Courtesy of the Fort Worth Star-Telegram):

> **American children rate bullying and teasing as their biggest problem**, *according to a survey of 8- to 15-year olds published in 2001 by the Kaiser Family Foundation. Studies have found that 15 to 25 percent of U.S. students are frequently bullied and that bullying and teasing seem to peak in middle school.*

To help protect your child against bullying, a recent public health bulletin offered this advice:

Bullying in schools has negative effects on the general school climate. Bullying also can have negative lifelong consequences for students who bully and for their victims. Here are some tips for parents:

If you are worried that your child is being bullied, get involved. Ask him or her directly. Parents are often unaware of the bullying problem and discuss it with their children on a limited basis. Students typically feel that adult intervention is infrequent and ineffective and that telling adults will only bring more harassment from bullies

Learn about the **signs and symptoms of bullying**. *A child may indicate by their behavior that he or she is being bullied. If your child shows some of the following signs, bullying may be responsible:*

1. *Your child is frightened of walking to and from school*
2. *Begs you to drive them to school*
3. *Is truant*
4. *Begins to do poorly in school*
5. *Comes home regularly with clothes or books destroyed*
6. *Refuses to talk about what is wrong*
7. *Has unexplained bruises, cuts, scratches*
8. *Begins to bully other children and/or siblings*
9. *Comes home starving (lunch or lunch money may have been stolen)*
10. *Becomes aggressive, disruptive or unreasonable*

Widening the Reach of "Sticks and Stones . . ."

Two principal tools bullies have always relied on are: Mocking and teasing. However, a newer and far more vicious threat has taken center stage in the bullies' arena, vastly increasing the target range. A recent news release addresses this (Reprint Courtesy of the Fort Worth Star-Telegram):

> Some children, now labeled **Cyber bullies**, *are using the Internet, cell phones and other high-tech mediums to torment and harass classmates.* The number of children engaged in this form of bullying is growing and the perpetrators are less likely to get caught since face-to-face confrontations can be bypassed.
> . . . *Although physical harm is rare, cyber bullying can be far more damaging psychologically than traditional bullying, experts say. . . . Cyber bullying creates a barrier between bullies and their victims, reducing the likelihood that the bullies will feel guilty about what they've done. . . . It can also bring out the bully in those you least expect. . . . The extreme cyber bullying cases that make headlines overshadow the minor ones that occur more often, such as forwarding private e-mails without the writer's permission or spreading rumors on message boards.*

"This is coming to a school near you," said Glen Stutzky, a Michigan State University professor of social work who studies school violence. "I think within the next year or two, it'll be a major issue."... *Many school districts have adopted rigid cell phone policies and have placed filters on school computers.*

Parents must work with school officials to stop this burgeoning menace, and it is important for parents to:

- Monitor their children's use of high-tech mediums at all times.
- Instruct their children in appropriate and responsible behavior; and teach them how to handle situations if they become targets of bullying.

More importantly, parents must model and teach their children a truly **Golden Rule:**

> *Do unto others as you would have them do unto you. (Paraphrased) Luke 6:31*

Meanwhile, Back at Home . . .

If children are upset with parents, their targets and verbal arrows shift: "I don't love you." Or, "I would rather be at Grandmother's house than here." Or, the old standby: "You love Kyle more than you love me." An especially hurtful remark is, "I will never forgive you for that!" Remember that words such as, "You can't make me," are an invitation to a power struggle that need not take place.

Never forget that you are the adult — the one in charge. Learn to regroup and quell your angry thoughts with positive coping statements before the thoughts become words that feed the anger flames. Speak calmly: You may feel you are losing a battle; but you may win or prevent a war by controlling your anger.

Memorize, use, and create other positive coping statements as outlined in Chapter 6: They are mind-shields against releasing torrents of verbal abuse, perpetuating angry encounters.

CHAPTER 2

"MAKING A LIST AND CHECKING IT TWICE..."

Sticky-notes spring up mushroom-like: On refrigerators, doors, mirrors, walls, and almost everywhere; they are a shorthand/ jot down version of lists and forms. Some of us have a built-in aversion to making detailed lists and filling out forms — which brings us to:

LISTS AND FORMS — "You Knew This Was Coming!"

Several lists and forms are included in this chapter and are provided for information. Their purpose is to aid you in setting up strategies for changes in your and your children's behavior. Choose to fill them out (use the shorthand/jot down approach — it works!) or to just review them.

"You Are Here..."

To determine where you and your child are now in terms of a starting point for changes to be made, review the need to collect baseline data. (A method of collection is shown below.)

The "Why" and "What For" of Baseline Data

The first step in changing problem behaviors is to *specifically define* the behavior so it can be counted. Parents tend to over-generalize and use global terms when they describe their children's problem behaviors. For example, they may say, "He's a lazy pig," instead of, "He leaves his clothes on the floor, his bed is not made, and his wet towel is left on the carpet." Instead of, "She's a monster!" say, "She hits, kicks, and bites."

Dr. G.R. Patterson (1976) reminds us of the importance of *defining behaviors in terms that can be counted.* Focusing on specific behaviors, instead of enduring traits, enables you to be more accurate in describing and counting how often your child's behavior actually occurs. Changing behaviors is easier than changing general traits. First, tell your child *exactly* what behavior you like or dislike. Then, follow with either *consistent* reinforcement or punishment. This will cause the behavior, over time, to more readily go up or down, respectively. *Name calling* does little more than provide negative attention (causing the undesired behavior to *increase*), hurt your child's self-esteem and impede a healthy, respectful bond.

Research shows that many parents of children with behavior problems have a negative bias, often reporting that their problem children engage in more negative behaviors than actually occur. Using a chart to pinpoint and count positive and negative behaviors (speaking clearly versus whining) allows you to accurately determine how often your child shows both positive and negative behavior.

Our tendency as parents (and as partners for that matter!) is to overlook the positive and overreact to the negative. This tendency may be at the root of your discipline problems. When our children are behaving appropriately, we often use the "Let well enough alone" approach. Essentially, we *ignore* their positive behavior. You will learn in Chapter 5 that ignoring a *negative* or *positive* behavior causes that behavior to decrease in frequency over time. We do want to *consistently* ignore some types of *negative* behaviors so that those behaviors decrease. But, consistently ignoring *positive* behaviors will also cause those behaviors to occur less often.

The ratio of parental praise versus negative comments made to children tends to be skewed toward the latter. Hearing mostly negative comments or commands may have a deleterious effect on the overall parent-child relationship. Parents often report (and kids, no doubt, will concur): "It seems as if all I do all day is to yell at and bark out orders to my kids." ("Pick up your messy room." "Don't bother your brother!") If they are honest, parents will report that at times they just don't like their child very much. And, the child who hears mostly negative, usually doesn't feel like warming up to Mom or Dad much either.

ACP will teach you how to tip the scale toward focusing more on the positive behaviors you want to see in your kids. As you provide more positive praise and attention and the desired positive behaviors increase (your child comes the first time you call), the opposite negative behaviors (ignoring you and not coming at all) will decrease. Focusing on increasing the positive reduces the need for more punishing consequences. *The best part about the ACP method is that the overall parent-child relationship becomes more loving!*

Collecting baseline data is an antidote to our negative tinged "glasses," allowing us to see objectively both our behavior and the behavior of our kids. Baseline data can identify the frequency of behaviors at the beginning and throughout the ACP program. If the negative behaviors do not decrease and the positive behaviors do not increase, you can evaluate what is going wrong with your program.

"Sounds Simple, But . . . Will I Take the Time?"

To Collect Baseline Data:

You can make a simple chart or use the Behavior Chart provided below.

- *For the first three days*, record every time you say something positive, neutral, or negative *toward the child you are having the most difficulty with*. You might be surprised by just how stingy you are with your praise! Dr. G. R. Patterson has noted that the person giving out the most positives receives the most positives. (You will be reminded of this often!) We have noticed in our clinical work that parent-child relationships, once strained and negative, quickly warm up as parents look for positive behaviors they can pay attention to and praise.
- *For the next five days,* monitor and record both positive *and* negative behaviors of the child you are working with. *Start with the child you are having the most difficulty with.*

1. Write child's name.
2. Write dates to record for one week.
3. Decide who will record — Mom and/or Dad or other caregiver.
4. Use the results of the **Positive Child Behavior Rating Form** below to identify three positive and three negative behaviors you can record.
5. Count the behavior each time it occurs and mark on the Behavior Chart.
6. Total behaviors daily and at the end of the week.
7. *Time-out or consequences are not used at this collection phase.*

√E CHILD BEHAVIOR RATING FORM

following is a list of positive child behaviors you might want
child to exhibit more often. **Rate how often the behavior
ently occurs from 1 (Hardly Ever), 2 (Sometimes), or 3
(**Frequently**). Use it often to keep track of where your child is at
now, and how they are changing.

POSITIVE CHILD BEHAVIOR RATING FORM

1. Gets up and is ready to go easily in the morning...1 2 3

2. Speaks in an appropriate voice without whining...1 2 3

3. Speaks in an appropriate voice without yelling...1 2 3

4. Is verbally respectful with siblings...1 2 3

5. Is verbally respectful with peers..1 2 3

6. Keeps hands to self, physically respects siblings...1 2 3

7. Keeps hands to self, physically respects others...1 2 3

8. Respects others' things...1 2 3

9. Takes proper care of his/her own things, toys, belongings, etc......................1 2 3

10. Finishes meals in a timely manner..1 2 3

11. Is well-behaved during meal time...1 2 3

12. Does what is asked the first time...1 2 3

13. Does what is asked without talking back..1 2 3

14. Talks with respect to adults..1 2 3

15. Controls anger reasonably/appropriately when told, "No"............................1 2 3

16. Can entertain his/herself for periods of time..1 2 3

17. Waits to talk or ask a question when adults/peers are talking........................1 2 3

18. Seems able to calm self down appropriately when upset.................................1 2 3

19. Gets ready, goes and stays in bed properly...1 2 3

20. Other...1 2 3

BEHAVIOR CHART SAMPLE

Child's Name: (Hazel)

Person(s) Recording Behavior: Mom

Dates: Feb 1st - Mon   through   Feb 7th - Sun

	Monday	Tuesday	Wednesday	Thursday	Friday	Saturday	Sunday
Positive Behaviors↓							
1. Talks without whining	√	√	√√	√	√	√	√
2. Asks for toy without grabbing, hitting, etc.	√√√	√√√√	√√√	√√√	√√√	√√√	√√√
3. Does what told, no talk back or disrespect	√√	√√√	√√√	√√	√	√√	√√
Total Positive Points→	9	11	11	9	7	9	10
Negative Behaviors↓							
1. Whines	√√√	√√√	√√√√	√√√	√√√	√√√√	√√√
2. Hits, bites, pushes, grabs	√	√√	√√	√√	√√	√√√	√
3. Talks back, disrespectful	√√√	√	√√	√	√	√	
Total Negative Points→	10	8	10	8	8	10	5
Grand Total *Positive Minus Negative Points*→	-1	+3	+1	+1	-1	-1	+5

10 – 3 = +7

Time-Out For:

1. hitting

2. talking back

3. whining

Consequences:

(Points)

+15 have a friend over

+10 play outside

+5   watch television

0   stay inside and do an extra chore

- 5   no cell phone

- 10 no CD player

- 15 no television or computer

BEHAVIOR CHART FORM

Child's Name: _____   Dates: _____ through _____

Person(s) Recording Behavior: _____

	Monday	Tuesday	Wednesday	Thursday	Friday	Saturday	Sunday
Positive Behaviors↓							
1.							
2.							
3.							
Total Positive Points→							
Negative Behaviors↓							
1.							
2.							
3.							
Total Negative Points→							
Grand Total *Positive Minus Negative Points→*							

Time Out For:

1.

2.

3.

Consequences:
(Points)
+15
+10
+ 5
  0
- 5
- 10
- 15

"A LITTLE BIT GOOD — A LITTLE BIT NAUGHTY"

Your Child's Temperament Style

Temperament is an individual's unique way of relating to the world. Temperament styles or predispositions are usually evident at birth. Parents of more than one child often report noticing differences in how their children react and relate to the environment. Certain temperament styles present varying discipline challenges and may require tailored interventions. However, the basics of parenting are the same regardless of your child's temperament: *Children need to experience they are valued and loved; children need to be taught to respect their parents and others, and to follow specific predetermined rules.*

"Directing? On Stage? In the Audience Clapping?"

In what role would your child feel most comfortable? Your child's temperament and personality are unique, but can be categorized to some extent. Clinical research has shown that some children appear to be more difficult or easier than others in terms of how they adapt to life. Some children are easy-going in terms of eating, sleeping, and responding to discipline, while others are more challenging.

Children's temperaments and personalities need to be considered when a discipline plan is developed. Learning how your child's temperament and personality interact with your temperament and personality and your discipline style allows you to set a more effective plan in motion. The process of teaching each child may vary depending on the child's individual temperament or personality. Consider the following three categories:

1. Difficult Children:

These children require a greater understanding of their environmental and emotional challenges, and need to learn how to modulate and cope with their feelings. Do not take their moodiness and overreactions personally; help them adjust rather than react to difficult situations. Difficult children seem to lack regularity in body functions, tend to withdraw from new objects or people, show intense reactions to stimulation, and have an overall negative disposition.

2. Shy Children:

These children have a low to moderate activity level, initial withdrawal from new objects or people, slow adaptation to changes in the environment, and mild intensity or reactions to stimulation. Let these children determine their own pace for joining in at play groups, saying "hello" or changing to a new activity. Give them ample opportunities to adapt to and cope with novelty, changes, and new experiences. Communicate confidence in their ability to grow in these challenging areas. Be a supportive anchor from which they can pivot. Do not personalize their need to take it slow as an indication of your failure as a parent.

Express your acceptance of your child as they mature and practice dealing with fears and anxieties; their self-confidence will grow. Let your child know that it is okay with you that they warm up slowly. They, in turn, will learn to accept themselves for who they are and accept and expand their capabilities. Though our culture values the "go-getter" and outgoing, self-assured child, communicate to your child that they are running their own race.

3. Easy Children:

Count your blessings! These children are generally the easiest to discipline. Nevertheless, be prepared for developmental milestones (entering kindergarten) that might cause your easygoing kid to throw tantrums, become moody and non-compliant. Easy children show regularity in body functions, a positive approach to a new object or person, are adaptable to changes in the environment, and have an overall positive disposition.

Take into consideration the following questions:

- Do I need to establish eye contact with my active child to insure he hears what I say?
- Will my shy child more likely join in if I encourage gently, rather than push him into a new social situation?

- Will my strong-willed child more likely obey when given choices, rather than when backed into a corner?

DISCIPLINE STYLE — Look for a Winning Pattern

Take inventory of your disciplinary style and *identify what works* and what needs to be changed:

- Do you resort to yelling when your children ignore your commands?
- Do you spank daily?
- How have these methods influenced your child's behavior?
- Do you make threats and then not follow-through?
- Do you remember to enforce punishment when it is given?
- Do you offer praise consistently for the child's behaviors you like?
- Has your daily yelling or verbal aggression caused aggressive behavior in your child?

Observe and learn how your child's behavior is affected when you forget to praise or when you are inconsistent in follow-through with appropriate punishment. And, learn to recognize how your words and actions influence your child's behavior.

RATING PARENTS' MOOD AND MARRIAGE

There May Be Thorns

When children arrive, a household's priorities necessarily change and a previous "rose garden" existence may cease to exist. Though parents love their children and enjoy watching them blossom on their paths to maturity, parents often lament the changes. Mothers, especially, appear to have difficulty coping. Research shows that Mothers tend to feel more depressed and experience more marital discord during their children's preschool years. In their troubled state, depressed Mothers may lash out at their children more frequently and may rate their children as having more behavior problems than they actually have.

Parenting can be difficult when you feel rested and at your best; effectively coping with children while you are tired and depressed may seem next to impossible. Determining your level of depression and pinpointing the origin of those feelings, can aid you in getting beyond your depressed feelings. (Information only: A copy of the

Beck Depression Inventory can be found on the Web at PsychCorp. com.)

Your relationship with your partner greatly influences your child's emotional and behavioral development. Children learn easiest through modeling. Your children will emulate how you interact with your partner. They will derive their self-esteem and present and future relationship behavior from observing how their parents treat one another. Identifying areas of your marriage that need strengthening is a productive move. (Information only: One way you can do this is by completing the Locke-Wallace Marital Adjustment Test, which can be accessed on the Web by entering: Locke-Wallace Marital Adjustment Test-Answer.)

"I DON'T HAVE A PROBLEM WITH ANGER — DO I?"

Consider the following: Do you find yourself getting angry often during the day? Perhaps you stay in a bad or irritable mood more often than not, and find that you attack others and complain about things for lengthy periods of time daily. If this scenario sounds familiar, try to determine why you feel this way. Perhaps there is an unresolved trauma or depression to be addressed. Are you dissatisfied with your marriage? Underlying issues such as these might be fueling your anger; if so, these issues need to be identified, understood, and resolved.

When you are angry, do you explode emotionally? Stuffing or hiding your feelings each time you're hurt or angry can lead to feelings of depression and anxiety. This information will help:

- **Expressing what you need and want leads to resolution of issues as they occur.**
- **Having more influence over the events in your life can lead to a greater feeling of power.**

Think about the following:

- Do your angry feelings cause you to think illogically and act impulsively?
- When you are angry do you play the event over and over in your mind, becoming angrier each time you think about what happened?
- You just can't seem to let go of the anger?

- Hanging on to daily things that make you angry keeps you primed to lose control. It's as if you're ready and waiting for the *straw to break the camel's back.*
- Does a minor mishap, such as your 3-year-old spilling juice, cause you to react angrily?

If you have a difficult time forgiving, forgetting, and resolving conflicts, you likely have a problem with anger. *Our kids do so many things daily that frustrate us, we must practice **rapid forgetting** or we may stay in a bad mood perpetually (primed to lash out).* Our young children may read our frustration and irritation as our disliking or, worse, hating them.

You may have a problem with anger if you frequently slap or spank your kids when they behave in a way you dislike. That is: Do you react physically more often than verbally? If so, then you may be at risk for abusing your child. Spanking often reinforces the parent since it gets immediate results. However, there are long-term negative consequences associated with chronic daily spanking.

Do your children appear to recoil when a mishap occurs, expecting a loud angry reaction from you? This can lead to your child avoiding your presence, especially as they get older. They may also be less inclined to open up and share their true feelings with you, fearing your angry wrath, critical judgment, or shaming. You might notice that your children have developed a short fuse by modeling your anger pattern. One indication is that they may be more impatient and lash out physically more than other kids their age.

The Lamphear Parent Anger Test (LPAT) follows. (Complete the test or review it.)

LAMPHEAR PARENT ANGER TEST

Complete the Lamphear Parent Anger Test (LPAT) below to identify what parent-child situations and events make you angry. Add the scores from the individual items to determine the extent of your anger problem.

Rate from 0 to 5 how angry the following events make you feel:

Not angry	A little angry	Somewhat angry	Angry	Very angry	Extremely enraged
0	1	2	3	4	5

1. _____Your 12-year-old asks if a friend can spend the night. You're exhausted from the hectic week and don't want to be kept up. She cries, "It's been a long time!" You are calm and in control as you make the first two responses. She keeps retorting with anger and sarcasm. The event seems to have no end.

2. _____You hand Amy a glass of juice and tell her to sit down at the table. When you turn around she is standing in the living room giving 18-month-old Carl "a sip." In a blink of an eye the drink is spilled all over Carl. It is in his eyes, up his nose, all over his new outfit, and down his freshly changed diaper. Carl is screaming and flailing about.

3. _____You finally got a new kitchen table after years of saving. After one week you notice deep pen-mark grooves on the wood surface.

4. _____You have been with the kids all day. You've given a lot and separated a lot of scuffles. Your husband gets home and you are excited to talk to him. You close the bedroom door and you hear, "Stop it! I had it first!" And then you hear a loud cry.

5. _____Driving home from the mall with your two children in the car, you feel exhausted. Finally, the baby goes to sleep and an angry 3½-year-old Lynn throws a toy which hits the baby. The baby wakes up screaming. You were planning on both kids falling asleep so that you could take a nap you desperately needed when you got home.

6. _____Five-year-old Sam wakes up at 2:00 a.m. coughing. You're exhausted, but get up to give him medicine. Sam slaps the spoonful of "yucky" medicine sending it flying all over you and the floor.

7. _____It's 3:00 a.m. and you're trying to give 2½-year-old Rachael her medicine. As you hold the spoonful of medicine, she won't open her mouth. After you ask her calmly and emphatically three times to open her mouth, she clenches it shut.

8. _____You are driving the children home from school on a hot day in busy traffic; Kimberly laughs at the picture Danny drew. Angered, Danny hits Kimberly. She hits him back. Now they're both screaming. Nothing you say works to calm them.

9. _____You wake up excited about the day planned at Disneyland and the fun the kids are going to have. Terry and John wake up cranky and start fighting over a toy. Neither boy wants the "special breakfast" you got up early to prepare.

10. _____You have bathed the kids and dressed them to get their Christmas picture taken. Four-year-old Jason sneaks some grape juice and spills it all over his only white shirt.

11. _____You are looking forward to the 30 minutes between 9:30 and 10:00 p.m. as *your* time after the kids are in bed. They get to bed on time but keep laughing and making noise. You reprimand them. It's 10:00 p.m. and they still need discipline. You realize there is no time left for you.

12. _____Finally, you have finished cleaning the house. A few of your old friends will be over in 10 minutes. You go upstairs to get ready. By the time you go back down, your three kids have created such a mess in the living room that it looks as though you have not cleaned it.

13. _____You tell your 4-year-old son it's time to go home from the park. He yells, "No!" With other parents watching the scene, you repeat your command. He runs away and screams, "I'm not leaving!"

14. _____You are feeling exhausted and edgy from a long, frustrating day at work and the 5:00 p.m. to 9:00 p.m. schedule with the kids alone. After you finally fall asleep, your 5-year-old wakes you and wants to sleep with you. He snores and moves and you can't get comfortable.

15. _____You are working on an important report for work that has to be completed by morning. Just as you think of

a good idea, your kids interrupt you, crying about who hit who first.

16. _____You are having lunch at a restaurant with a friend you've not seen for a long time. Your toddler won't sit in his seat. Every time you try to talk or listen, the baby starts to cry, throws his food, or tries to "escape."

17. _____You are running late for school and work. Six-year-old Tina says the seam in her socks "doesn't feel right." The next pair you give her "bother her, too" and so do the next three pairs. Finally, she falls on the floor and cries. Your other two kids still aren't dressed.

18. _____Your 2½-year-old first born clings to you at the play group and can't seem to fit in with the other children. The other kids are laughing and having fun. You assume that the other parents think there is something wrong with your son.

19. _____After a year of weekly practice, your 7-year-old still comes in last in the swim races.

20. _____You are visiting friends you haven't seen for years. Your 10-year-old insists on wearing his green striped shirt, his orange checkered shorts, and his oldest pair of shoes.

21. _____It's 5:30 a.m., and you are sleeping soundly. Your 3-year-old comes into your bed. You hope, *"He'll fall back asleep and so will I;"* but he doesn't. He keeps whining for you to get up. You are exhausted deep down to your bones and worried about how you'll perform when you go to work in a few hours.

22. _____It's 7:00 a.m. and you're rushed for time. It's the third time in five minutes that you've re-done the hair of your 9-year-old and she screeches again, "Not like that! The hairs are all sticking up!"

23. _____It's 3:00 p.m. The house is still a mess and you hate how dirty it looks. All you've done is try to "survive" and keep your head above water tending to your 5- and 2-year-olds, and 6-month-old. Your shoe soles stick in spots as you walk across the kitchen floor.

24. _____You gather all the cleaning materials to deep-clean the

shower. You've begun and had to stop four times in order to discipline your bickering teens.

25. _____Danny started kindergarten. He cried before, during, and after school for the first week and threw a tantrum when you tried to leave. He had been confident and independent and had no problem separating at preschool. You fear he won't adjust and that something might be wrong with him socially, and with the way you've raised him.

26. _____You have just painted your nails for a special night out with friends. Four-year-old Sean is overly playful and accidentally smears your polished nails. You don't have time to repaint them.

27. _____It's 5:00 p.m. and you just mopped the kitchen floor, anticipating your husband's delight that the kitchen "looks nice." You leave for a moment, walk back in and notice mud tracks from the back door across the kitchen floor and onto the carpet in the den.

28. _____You have reminded 8-year-old Anna to get dressed three times. Five minutes before you need to leave, you glance into her room, hoping she's ready. She's still playing with her toys and has not begun to dress.

29. _____You have only 20 minutes to shop for stockings you need for a wedding and formula for the baby. Once in the store, 3-year-old Ashley takes her stroller belt off, climbs out, and runs away. She hides in the clothes racks and you can't find her. The store clerk and other parents are staring at you.

30. _____You have taken 11-year-old Audrey to school and she is getting out of the car very slowly. You're already 10 minutes late to work.

31. _____You are trying to concentrate on a difficult work project; your teenagers are clowning around. They are making a lot of noise; you're sure the horseplay will escalate and someone will get hurt.

32. _____You made a mistake at work and you feel insecure and down. At 9:30 p.m., your daughter tells you she has a math test tomorrow, and she has not studied the material.

33. _____You are tired and stressed. Your 4-year-old is flinging his arms in protest to getting his pajamas on and hits you in the nose.

34. _____You are starving! You tell your 6-year-old "no" to buying gum at the grocery store check-out stand. He screams and cries and hits you as you stand for 10 minutes in a slow line.

Scoring the Lamphear Parent Anger Test

Add the ratings for each question for a grand total score. Next, check your score against the scale below. Notice which items you marked with a value of 3, 4, or 5 to determine which incidents are most likely to trigger your anger.

Scale for range of parent anger:

0 – 35	Normal
36 – 70	Mild
71 – 104	Moderate
105 – 139	Serious; counseling indicated
140 – 175	Very Serious; counseling indicated

"KEEP A GOOD RECORD . . ." — Daily Anger Record Instructions

Recording daily anger events, along with your thoughts and expectations regarding the events, makes it easier to understand and change your anger pattern. The Daily Anger Record provides a format for this. Your best results are gained by completing the record daily. (For convenience you may want to make several copies of the form.) This is an efficient way to identify the situations and behaviors involving your children that make you angry. Especially, pay attention to the *automatic thoughts* you have during the event. Your thoughts reveal the meaning and expectations you have (what you think should happen) regarding your child's negative behaviors. To effect change, look for and analyze patterns in your meanings and expectations. Often these patterns relate to past, unresolved issues.

If you choose to keep a Daily Anger Record, the format is simple:

- Describe the anger event.
- Describe the thoughts you had during and after the anger event.
- Record your expectations, the meaning the behavior has for you, and a more objective view of the situation.

OVERVIEW: Describing your thoughts is the most important step since it allows you to identify the *automatic thoughts* you have during the event. These thoughts reflect the meaning and the expectations you have regarding your child's negative behaviors. Slowing down your automatic thoughts so that you can monitor your self-talk (what you are "saying" to yourself) is an important first step toward better anger management. Following this approach allows you to rewrite a more objective view of the situation and you will notice that you feel less angry.

Daily Anger Record Sample

DATE: February 4th

1. BRIEF ACCOUNT OF EVENT:

Siblings fighting
Disrespectful talking
Climbs on counter

2. THOUGHTS DURING EVENT:

"Every time I try to read, the little brats get into a fight!"
"He talks like that just to upset me."
"He is climbing on the counter just to get my attention; he knows he isn't supposed to do that! He does it just to get me mad."

3. HOW ANGRY DID YOU FEEL DURING THE EVENT: (CIRCLE ONE)

(1 = not very angry to 10 = very angry)

1   2   3   4   **5**   6   7   8   9
10

4. FOR EACH THOUGHT IN #3 INDICATE YOUR EXPECTATIONS THAT DIDN'T GET MET AND/OR WHAT YOUR CHILD'S BEHAVIOR MEANT ABOUT YOU.

- I expected to have my kids obey every time I sit down to read.
- My son wants to upset me; he doesn't care how I feel; I expect him to care about me.
- I expect that my son should never climb on the counter; my son doesn't care if I get upset.

5. WRITE A MORE OBJECTIVE VIEW OF THE SITUATION BY IDENTIFYING YOUR THINKING DISTORTIONS (Discussed in Chapter 5) AND RE-WRITING YOUR THOUGHTS.

Over-generalizing and Labeling: They don't fight *every time* I read. They *aren't* brats. They need to be disciplined even if I am reading. I just wish they'd fight less. I need to go back to the point system to train them to resolve differences properly.

Mind reading: I don't know *what* my son is thinking, or why he is talking disrespectfully or, for that matter, if he cares if I'm upset. I need to take away points for disrespectful talk and not take his behavior so personally.

Mind reading and Personalizing: He's just two-years-old; he shouldn't be caring about my feelings; that's unrealistic! He is getting on the counter because I have been inconsistent in my response to him. I need to use the chart and time-out to teach him he will lose points and the things he enjoys if he climbs on the counter.

6. AS YOU LOOK BACK ON THE EVENT NOW, HOW MUCH ANGER DO YOU FEEL?

I   2   3   4   5   6   7   8   9
IO

Daily Anger Record Form
DATE: _____
1. BRIEF ACCOUNT OF EVENT:

2. THOUGHTS DURING EVENT:

**3. HOW ANGRY DID YOU FEEL DURING EVENT? :
(CIRCLE ONE)**
(1 = not very angry to 10 = very angry)
1   2   3   4   5   6   7   8   9
10

4. FOR EACH THOUGHT IN #3 INDICATE EXPECTATIONS THAT DIDN'T GET MET AND/OR WHAT YOUR CHILD'S BEHAVIOR MEANT ABOUT YOU:

5. WRITE A MORE OBJECTIVE VIEW OF THE SITUATION BY IDENTIFYING YOUR THINKING DISTORTIONS AND REWRITING YOUR THOUGHTS.

6. AS YOU LOOK BACK ON THE EVENT NOW, HOW MUCH ANGER DO YOU FEEL?
1   2   3   4   5   6   7   8   9
10

Anger Provoking Situations — Hierarchy Form
Look at your Daily Record Forms for the week.
Complete the following exercises after you have recorded several forms.
A. Make a list of 10 things you found that made you angry and score them as:
(1 = a little angry to 10 = very angry).

1. _____

2. _____

3. _____

4. _____

5. _____

6. _____

7. _____

8. _____

9. _____

10. _____

B. Now arrange the following with #1 as the event or situation that makes you the least angry and #10 the angriest.

1. _____

2. _____

3. _____

4. _____

5. _____

6. _____

7. _____

8. _____

9. _____

10. _____

What did you learn about your anger issues?

RELAXATION MOTIVATORS

Relaxation is not the same thing as falling in bed, exhausted, and immediately going to sleep. When you are physically and mentally tense and stressed, your body is primed for aggression and fighting. If you hear noises and think an intruder is in your house, your heart pounds, you tense up, and your body prepares for flight or fight. When your body is in a chronic state of tension with elevated adrenalin (in the absence of a real threat), you are at risk to suffer hypertension and other serious medical disorders. Also, you are prone to lash out verbally and physically at minor annoyances.

Our children constantly challenge our patience and self-control. Successive incidents accumulate, causing us to tense up and feel irritated, frustrated and annoyed. ***Learning to release tension as it occurs is imperative to anger control.*** If tension builds and is repressed or stuffed, you may fail to control your temper during a minor incident such as a child accidentally spilling milk or dropping a plate, or not responding promptly to instructions.

However, the effects of stress on our children must also be considered. Though we tend to view stress as a condition exclusive to adults, research shows this is not so. We often expect our young children to act "grown-up" as we urge them to get higher grades, excel in extracurricular activities — often of our choice — and score perfectly on tests. Such expectations and demands create a stress-inducing environment for all family members.

According to a recent survey of nearly 900 children between the ages of 9 and 13 conducted by KidsHealth, a division of Nemours Foundation, a nonprofit that studies children's health issues:

More than four in 10 kids surveyed said they feel stressed most of the time or always. They cited having too much to do as the main reason. Dr. Kate Cronan, medical editor for the KidsHealth Web site, cited extracurricular activities as the main culprits.
Three severe consequences of stress include:
- *loss of sleep,*
- *falling behind in school, and*
- *burnout.*

Additionally, kids must contend with stresses at home and cope with often insensitive peers at school. Expert opinions differ on whether today's kids face more stress than ever before, but it appears beyond dispute that younger children are exhibiting anxiety patterns usually associated with older kids and grown-ups. These patterns include:
- Insomnia
- Skin eruptions/disorders
- Headaches
- Queasy stomachs
- Depression.

A compelling motive for learning and practicing anger control is: Child care professionals have determined that children often copy the tendency to get stressed-out from their parents/caregivers. It is important to understand that: **Relaxation is an essential health aid for all family members.**

Learning to relax is a skill that takes practice. Developing the ability to stay calm during a disciplinary challenge reassures your child that you know how to stay in control mentally, physically, and behaviorally. You will develop a history of self-control: The memory of remaining calm and in control will increase your confidence as a disciplinarian.

If appropriate, considering ages and temperaments of your children, you might include them in a modified version of the breathing exercise that follows. Studies show that children benefit from learning and practicing calming techniques and breathing exercises could prove helpful.

DEEP BREATHING

Deep breathing is an important and natural way to relax physically. The basic procedure is to slowly deep breathe in through your nose (to the count of 1-2-3-4), hold your breath (to the count of 1-2), and exhale slowly through your mouth (to the count of 1-2-3-4-5-6). (Pretend that you are blowing out a candle.) This allows more oxygen into the lungs and causes the chest and other upper body processes to relax. Breathe in a manner that is comfortable for you. We have a tendency to swallow air, especially when faced with stress or when we're angry. This can lead to greater tension, especially evidenced by tightness in the chest.

Inhaling a slow, deep breath, holding it and exhaling relaxes your chest muscles and extends a calm peacefulness throughout your body. You will be more relaxed, less stressed, and less angry. You cannot be tense with stress and anger and relaxed at the same time. (If you include children in the exercises: You might change the counts to 1-2 on both inhaling and exhaling. Do not overtax the children. Make their sessions short.)

Practice deep, calm breathing throughout the day: For example, each time you take a sip of a beverage, stop at a traffic signal, or go to the restroom.

STAGES OF RELAXATION

The ability to relax quickly and deeply is an essential tool in anger management. Acquiring that skill involves three successive levels. ***(ACP provides relaxation CDs for each of these levels.)***

Progressive Relaxation:

To achieve progressive relaxation, each of the major muscle groups is alternately tensed and relaxed. The purpose of this exercise: To learn to notice the difference between tenseness and relaxation. When you feel tense, it is a cue for you to relax. As with other skills, the more you practice the quicker and deeper you will go into relaxation. With practice, you will strengthen neural connections of relaxation. With frequent practice, you can relax on cue.

Relax Only:

Develop this skill after two weeks of practicing Progressive Relaxation. Scan your body mentally from head to toe (as if you are looking with your mind's eye), and give your muscles the command to "relax" or "let go." Focus especially on the tight areas, the places you tense up the most and where you harbor your anger and anxiety.

Mental Imagery:

This skill follows the Relax Only phase. During this stage, you will learn to relax quickly while listening to a soothing relaxation tape or when conjuring a pleasant scene or circumstance. As you systematically practice relaxing you will notice how easy it is for you to relax on command.

Reminder: Throughout the relaxation procedures, it is essential that you use slow, deep breathing. This will enhance the relaxation effect. *(The ACP relaxation CDs will teach you to relax on cue.)*

CHAPTER 3

"PIED PIPERS . . ."

To fully understand your children's emotions and behavior you need to assess several areas of influence. In addition to child temperament and parents' discipline styles, other significant social, cultural and parental factors impact a child's current *and* long-term adjustment. Discussion of these issues can be controversial and difficult to consider. Our intent is not to arouse guilt or assign blame. I share this information with you both as a parent and clinical psychologist so that you can make more informed decisions about your child's psychosocial development.

Parents must realize that pervasive harmful influences are acting as Pied Pipers, and are ensnaring the hearts and minds of their children. The tune is mesmerizing and children will follow blindly unless given *effective and consistent* parental direction and guidance.

CULTURAL AND SOCIAL FACTORS: Television and Movies — "24/7"

For years, we drifted along with the changing flow of content in television and movies, without much thought of the direction being taken. We may have noted that we were enjoying the journey less and maybe now and then we thought good programs and movies were more difficult to find. We may even have thought: *This doesn't affect me; if I don't like it, I don't have to watch it.* But there was and is much more at stake.

Now, we look about, startled to find the flow has taken us to stagnant backwaters reeking of explicit sexual and violent material. Worse yet, viewer demands have turned these backwaters presentations into mainstream fare on primetime airtime and at most movie theaters. We can only imagine the harmful long-term effects on society — especially on our young ones.

Since the 1980s we have witnessed an alarming and steady increase in the amount of sexual themes and violence to which our children are exposed. Many primetime situation comedies (sitcoms) and popular movies depict children cast in sexual roles and talking or hearing about sexual issues at earlier ages than ever before. With our children caught in this swirl of negative and harmful influences from multiple sources, why are we so shocked when we hear that the average age kids first have sex is twelve years-old? Daily exposure to sexual themes, from television, billboards, video games, in the music they listen to, in the chat rooms they participate in, and on *My Space,* as well as risqué and violent commercials during G-rated shows, is routine for our youth. Easy Internet access is a click away for most kids at their or a friend's home, on their or a friend's cell phone, iPod or BlackBerry.

A study released in 2001 revealed that the sexual content of primetime sitcoms, often watched by young children and teens, increased 30% over the previous year. In 2005 a similar study indicated that sexual content of primetime sitcoms continued to climb steadily. Results of the studies show clearly that such graphic presentations adversely affect these vulnerable viewers.

Recently, researchers surveyed 1,792 12- to 17-year-olds nationwide about their TV viewing habits and sexual experience. There were two surveys conducted about one year apart. Both surveys concluded that:

> *While factors such as age, older friends, lower grades and rule-breaking behavior were associated with the timing of initial sexual intercourse,* **television had the strongest effect.** (Emphasis added.)

We must acknowledge our responsibility as parents in addressing and changing the onslaught of negative cultural elements and mediums impacting our children's development. As a parent, I often have felt overwhelmed and powerless against the rising tide of negative sludge my kids wade through. We cannot, however, give up or stay complacent. For our *children's* sake, we must become more aware of the deluge of inappropriate material bombarding our children and demand accountability by those responsible.

The following information provides a glimpse of the *persistent* pursuit of our children by the entertainment industry, too often spurred by greed and power:

- In 2004, editors at Merriam-Webster approved the inclusion of *teensploitation* in the annual update of their Collegiate Dictionary.
- Teensploitation is defined as: *The exploitation of teen-agers by the producers of teen-oriented films.*

It typically takes 20 years of mainstream media use for a word to earn consideration for placement in an abridged dictionary. Twenty years! The first sighting of the word *teensploitation* should have sent shock waves throughout society. Parents/caregivers and teachers must work together to form a protective shield around our teens and children while stringent measures are taken to eliminate this ugly practice.

Children and teens relentlessly insist on:

- viewing unsuitable films,
- attending questionable music concerts,
- attending parties with no (or questionable) chaperones, and
- spending leisure time at places parents deem unsuitable.

Alarmed parents react by resisting and denying permission.

This *insistence/resistance cycle* creates family conflicts that are numerous and frequent and often include heated confrontations. At times, as anger levels rise, physical abuse becomes a part of the battles. Family harmony is ruptured as children devise endless methods to persuade parents to allow them access to off-limits venues. When their entreaties fail, many children find ways to bypass parental authority.

For parents, the task of supervising and safeguarding their children continues to grow more demanding, more frustrating, and more important. Anger flares high as parents try to protect their young ones and are met with stubborn opposition and accusations such as: "You don't remember what it's like to be young!" "You never want me to have fun!" "You don't trust me!" "You're so old fashioned. Times have changed!"

Yes, times have changed and the trend is troubling: There is a shrinking supply of acceptable, healthy forms of family entertainment. Remember when any children's movie was classified automatically as a *safe* movie for children and families? G-rated movies were thought of as synonymous with family/children's entertainment. Now, parents need to review movies and television programs carefully before allowing their children access. Many are rife with inappropriate sexuality, erotic themes and too many instances depicting pain and cruelty toward others. Some *children's* movies have overly terrifying characters and events which are inappropriate for young children who are the primary audience targets.

Many PG-rated movies with teenage and adult themes are marketed to children less than 8-years-old. Our young children watch them repeatedly, soaking their minds with the possibly harmful themes and images. Am I blasting the movie industry? No. I am agreeing: Indeed, times have changed. And I am emphasizing that the changes, more often than not, are having a negative impact on families. Parents often say, "You can't shield kids from what's out there." Adopting that stance allows the inappropriate material to flow more freely. Decisive action by parents and caregivers can help stem this tide.

As shown by recent surveys, escalating sexual exposure heavily contributes to today's kids engaging in sex at preteen ages. If we remain silent and unresponsive to this critical situation, we contribute to damaging consequences for our kids, including the higher risk for AIDS. On an equally scary note, media material depicting kids and adults killing each other is rampant and escalating. Survey results released in 2004 show:

- *A typical child in the U.S. watches 28 hours of TV a week and sees 8,000 murders by the time he finishes elementary school. Even worse, the killers get away with the crime 75% of the time and show no remorse.*
- *The result? Some kids become immune to brutality, some become fearful, and others become aggressive.*

Along with monitoring the types of TV shows and video games their children view, parents must also pay attention to commercials sandwiched between *primetime* programs. Often there are adult ads for sexually explicit or violent daytime and evening programs as well as adult-themed commercial products. An ever increasing number of shows on television today feature men and women undressing and making sexual overtures in situations which undermine family life and family values.

More than 850,000 worried Americans have joined the Parents Television Council (PTC). The conservative leaning PTC rates shows to indicate violence, foul language or sexual content. It also pushes networks to move explicit shows to later time slots. (Visit www.parentstv.org for more information.)

TANGLED TENTACLES OF THE COMPUTER AND INTERNET

As parents, we are frightened by our children's ease of access to decadent and immoral material via the Internet. Though you may have controls on your computer to shield your children, as noted above kids have easy access to the Internet on their or a friend's cell phone, watch, iPod, or BlackBerry. An increasingly common occurrence is exposure to adult sexual themes and the popping up of pornographic material when our children are on the Internet.

An increasingly serious concern centers on Internet chat rooms which continue to proliferate and send out far-reaching tentacles in every direction day and night. Kids are especially susceptible to a chat room approach because it appears exciting and "safe" to them. However, a seemingly innocuous chat room "conversation" can quickly turn into a sexually themed dialogue. Adult addiction to cyber sex is a growing problem and child addiction appears to be following that alarming trend. Media reports confirm and emphasize: *What often begins as curiosity frequently ends in disaster*.

Many law enforcement agencies have added special Cyber Crimes Units to their departments. More stringent laws governing inappropriate use of computers and the Internet are being enacted and enforced. The term "inappropriate use" is being replaced by "illegal use" and allows a small foothold of legal remedies in the persisting effort to protect our children. However, rapidly changing and emerging technology requires that laws be constantly updated, enacted, and enforced to close loopholes exploited by many lawyers to the detriment of the general citizenry. Parents must learn more about the dangers stemming from the gross abuse of the Internet and the harmful effects and influences that medium can have on their children. Parents will then readily see the urgent need to devise methods to protect their children.

WAYS TO PROTECT YOUR CHILDREN:

- Teach kids not to give out personal information.
- Tell them not to agree to a face-to-face meeting with someone they met online.
- Tell kids never to respond to messages that make them feel uncomfortable and to report such messages to you.
- Place computers in a public room where they can be monitored.
- Establish ground rules, including when kids can use the Internet and what sites they can visit.
- Learn about parental controls and archiving features. (Source: Texas Attorney General's Cyber Crimes Unit)

In another venue, the *virtual reality* of the computer video games replete with *blood and guts* allows children to experience *killing someone, dismembering them,* and *blowing them to bits.* Research shows this type experience desensitizes children to killing in the *real world.* Such exposures may cause a child who has serious emotional, social, and family problems to become even more fragile emotionally.

The ultimate goal of the media is to get their messages out to the widest possible audience, particularly in the marketing of products. Movies, video games, and advertising are multi-billion dollar industries. What connection does today's prevailing violence have to these lucrative markets? Though it is disheartening, there is a simple explanation: *Supply and demand.* The American public and media are apparently fascinated by viewing, writing, and reading about violence.

Ideally, the demand factor would be removed by stopping the supply. However, with multi-billion dollar industries involved and pitted against anyone threatening that income flow, battle lines will be difficult to establish. And the battle will require the joining of forces and all the resources parents and caregivers and others can muster. The outcome is critical: The welfare of our nation's youth is at stake. **We must get involved, stay involved, and stay committed.**

A tiny light signaling change flickers in the darkness of negative teen statistics, and may be attributed to growing parental awareness, concern, and involvement. A report issued July 16, 2004, by the Federal Interagency Forum on Child and Family statistics, shows:

- *The teenage birth rate — steadily declining since 1991 — hit a record low in 2002.*
- *Young people were less likely to be victimized in a serious violent crime — murder, rape, robbery or aggravated assault — or to commit one.*

Despite these findings, the ages of child murderers and their victims keep dropping and the circumstances surrounding such incidents are increasingly bizarre.

Pushing the Envelope Has Become More Dangerous

There is nothing new about teens pushing to see and do things to which their parents object. Today, however, *the ways teens may choose to rebel* are not only more damaging emotionally and physically, they can be deadly. Many drugs are extremely potent, highly addictive, and *more easily accessible* than in years past. Increasingly casual sex by pre-teen aged children could result in a life-time of disease or even death from AIDS. Our overindulged teens constantly seek more outrageous forms of excitement and entertainment. Despite their getting *more* of what they *want,* depression and suicide rates among teens and children continue to climb.

Parents must act to insure that the pendulum swings back to the basics that nurture healthy development in our kids; for example:

- Having a stable family home life
- Being assigned reasonable chores
- Having reasonable expectations
- Enjoying simple pleasures
- Learning to delay gratification

LOOK CLOSELY AT FAMILY ENVIRONMENT AND VALUES

If someone asked you to describe your family environment and values, how would you answer? Parents must consider values they want to instill in their children and then teach, enforce, and model those values. Surprisingly, few parents have carefully thought this process through. ***Know this: If you don't instill appropriate values in your children, you leave them open to accepting and practicing***

questionable values from other sources. This critical step in your family's development gains importance considering your children's daily exposure to harmful cultural and peer influences.

Some thought points are:

- Do you model and emphasize a strong spiritual influence in your family?
- Do you expect and demand that your children show respect for the rights of others?
- Do you model and emphasize respecting the rights and boundaries of others?
- Are your children allowed to use slang in a sarcastic way, such as "Yeah, right!" Or, do you insist that they talk to you and others with respect?
- Do you model respectful talk between spouses?

Children learn by example and are more willing to listen when parents model the behavior they expect from their children. Take time to review your family environment:

- Do both parents work?
- How tense and hectic is the daily routine?
- Does your child internalize or externalize the family tension?
- Do the kids have enough time to just relax and share whatever is on their minds or is the family always "on the go" with everyone feeling constantly rushed?
- Does your family show visible love and warm encouragement among family members?
- What is the tone of the family?
- Is there yelling and screaming or mostly positive communication?
- Do you listen to each other?
- Is everyone given opportunities to be heard?

TOO MUCH PRESSURE TOO LITTLE TIME

Children and teenagers today often complain that they don't have enough down-time, and say they feel as if they are constantly meeting a deadline or schedule. At a time when families are at risk for breaking up (the divorce rate is climbing close to 60%), kids are participating in so many extra-curricular activities that family dinners and family-times have become traditions of the past. Parents often report, "But my kids like to be involved in a lot of activities." Still, it is our responsibility as parents to determine what is best for the whole family and not focus exclusively on individual desires.

Maintaining a relaxing home environment where family can just relax together and have time to share about their day is the glue that forms a cohesive and loving bond. I believe we need to safeguard our precious family time. This might require letting go of the pull for our kids to get an early start in sports and other extra-curricular activities.

On the topic of pressure, Dr. David Elkind warns us about the fallout of "the hurried child." Preschoolers aren't the only ones pressured to excel at earlier and earlier ages. A recent trend is to encourage high school teens to take as many college level (AP) courses as possible during high school. This move increases their chances to be more competitive in college acceptance and to "shave off" a year of college. Basically, we are encouraging our kids to give up precious high school social time so they can graduate earlier from college, and, what, start working one year earlier?

Every child is different and for some this approach may fit. But I am concerned about the rising number of stressed out teenagers in my clinical practice who are trying to meet what, for many, are unhealthy and even harmfully high standards. They have the rest of their lives to work, but only four short years to participate in and enjoy high school life.

Other complaints I often hear from kids is that they feel lonely and that they don't see their parents often enough. Typically, each family member has a TV and computer in their room: This further reduces family togetherness and sharing and creates a greater sense of isolation and alienation. Results from a recent longitudinal study of current American child adjustment echo the concerns discussed above and yielded surprising results. Children from upper middle-income level homes ($125,000 or more annual income) are generally presumed to be at *low risk* for adjustment problems compared to their lower-income level counterparts. However, Luthar (2003) and others found that the kids from upper-income level homes are reporting *higher rates* of substance abuse, depression, and anxiety than their lower-income level peers.

Luthar and her colleagues identified two potential causes for the rising rates of problems among affluent youth: (1) excessive pressure to achieve and (2) little time with parents, primarily the Mother. This trend emphasizes the run-away-train of "enough is never enough" and the injurious effects on our affluent children. Answers to the complex question of the overall value of both parents working are not easy to define. For single parents, often there is no other choice except a full work week. But the end results of that arrangement on children deserve our attention and amplify the need to mitigate any negative effects on the children's development and future well-being.

Clearly, the fallout of our pursuit for "more" meaning and money coupled with pressure on kids to excel and less time with Mom is becoming more difficult to justify. As parents we need to take a more informed look at how our choices are affecting our children. Yes, psychologists can develop programs to help our kids "cope" with the decisions we make that aren't the best for their long-term development. However, I would like to see more time and resources devoted to prevention of the problems that develop. Administering Band-Aid corrections as cover-ups after the fact is no solution.

One positive influence that can be stressed and put into practice is requiring participation of family members at mealtimes as often as possible:

> *Results of a new study report released in 2004 suggests that teens that eat five to six meals (breakfast, lunch or dinner) per week with their families are less likely to have emotional, academic and substance-abuse problems than kids who don't.*

You might want to reflect on the following:

- Is my child depressed, anxious or aggressive because she needs more attention from me?
- Would my child benefit from being home more hours with a parent or from the material things a second income can provide?
- Is our family so much "on the go" that we rarely just sit together and enjoy each other?

- How much time do I allocate to teach and discipline my children each day?
- How can we reduce the escape into TV and technology and increase family time?
- Have I articulated the values and spiritual beliefs that I want my children to absorb?

"FOR BETTER OR WORSE . . ." — Your Marital Relationship

The quality and stability of your relationship with your spouse or partner is, perhaps, the single most important long-term influence on your children. You should:

- Show each other visible respect, love, and affection.
- Talk to each other politely.
- Not yell at and put each other down sarcastically in the presence of the children.
- Demonstrate how to problem solve effectively.
- Communicate effectively.
- Be quick to forgive.

The perceived parental bond critically impacts a child's sense of security and self-esteem. When love is openly demonstrated daily by family members, a child feels a greater sense of security. *Children learn how to love others by the way they are loved and by how their parents show love for one another*. Divorced parents must take special care to consider their children's feelings and to demonstrate mutual respect and speak to and of each other in a caring way.

Research shows a significant relationship between children's socio-emotional development and parents' marital relationships. Especially important is the extent to which the Father supports and encourages the Mother, which influences how the Mother relates to the child. Children of all ages can sense marital discord and will often act out to reduce the perceived tension. In an attempt to change the marital relationship, children may become more aggressive or strive to behave perfectly. This type pressure can overwhelm a child and, more importantly, a child is not emotionally equipped to bear this tremendous burden. Nor should they have to!

With *the divorce rate approaching 60% nationally and being even higher for second marriages* with children; wise couples are seeking marital counseling every few years. This preventive approach allows pent up resentments and misunderstandings to be identified and resolved. Problem solving and communication skills can be honed. **When I ask my child clients, "What is one thing you wish your parents would do differently?" The answer given most often is "Not yell so much," and the answer often includes a specific: "Not argue so much."**

The best lifetime gift we can give to our children is healthy exposure to a happy, functional marriage. Though most children hope to live and share life with both parents in one home, this is not always possible. However, even under adverse circumstances, parents and caregivers can work together to insure that children feel secure and cherished.

IS DIVORCE REALLY THAT BAD ON KIDS?

Put Down That Paint Brush! Evidence from a recent groundbreaking study suggests that we can no longer whitewash the devastating effects of divorce on kids. In the book, *The Unexpected Legacy of Divorce*, Dr. Wallerstein and her colleagues describe the results of their recent 25-year landmark study (Wallerstein, Lewis and Blakeslee, 2000). These world renowned researchers clearly document the negative effects on children stemming from divorce. They found the deleterious impact of the divorce experience is cumulative and continues long into adulthood. Validating earlier studies, they found that: Compared to their non-divorced counterparts, children of divorce experience "on average" more serious social, behavioral, academic, and economic problems.

As divorced children approach adolescence and young adulthood, they may have more difficulty connecting emotionally. They sometimes are afraid to love, exhibit emotional closeness, or to trust and marry. Children of divorce may fear abandonment and expect *their* marriages to fail. Surveys find they often leave the marriage first to avoid being left. Moreover, incidents of divorce are higher for children whose parents divorced, making it doubly important that we learn how to create and sustain a healthy marriage relationship for the sake of our children.

Current research points to the complex interplay of individual, parental, pre-divorce and economic factors in influencing post-divorce child adjustment. Parental cooperation, attention to the children's needs, continued involvement of both parents and economic resources seem to positively influence the outcome for kids. Still, simple common sense evaluation suggests that divorce is not *optimal* for the psychosocial development of children.

Clearly, in cases of physical and emotional abuse, high conflict marriages, addictions and the like (approximately 25% of divorces), divorce can provide a viable solution. But 60% of married couples who seek a divorce each year do not fit into this category. Many couples appear to adopt the attitude condoned by our current culture: "I do ... until it doesn't make *me* happy anymore." When children are involved, such an egocentric decision seems unfair. That children can be counted on to *adapt or cope* with divorce seems equally unfair.

In part to mitigate parental guilt and anxiety, some argue that children are *resilient* and can *survive* adverse consequences of divorce. As a parent and child psychologist, I would argue that such an attitude gets us off the hook for putting our needs (or wants) above our children's needs. I believe *all* children deserve much more than *surviving* the negative environment their society and parents thrust upon them. Professionals have scurried to develop much needed intervention programs to help children of divorce *cope* with the trauma they often experience. Demonstrating that these programs can mitigate the adverse effects of divorce seems to be a cultural validation of divorce being as acceptable as lasting marriages.

Wouldn't our children be better served if we put our focus on *divorce prevention* and putting *the children's needs first*? It is clear that divorce, like daycare for preschoolers, is not optimal for our children's long-term emotional development. It may be politically incorrect to voice that opinion, but facts speak loudly in support of seeking avenues other than divorce. Wallerstein's in-depth conversations with hundreds of divorced children, in conjunction with other studies, suggest that the emotional scars of the divorce process are not easily overcome.

Also, parents need to be aware that:

According to a 2005 study by researchers from the University of Chicago and Duke University, the stress of divorce and its aftermath have health consequences that may not show up for years.

Marital research has shown that identifying sources of frequent conflict and disagreement, practicing effective problem solving, and showing love and respect for one another can strengthen and increase mutual satisfaction in a marital relationship. Scheduling periodic counseling may help you come to terms with any past or present issues adversely affecting your marriage and family.

Unfortunately, couples often seek professional help after the relationship has deteriorated to such an extent that it is difficult to catapult it forward. By contrast, regular counseling check-ups can lead to or sustain healthy and mutually satisfying marriages. Moreover, you allow your children to witness how partners respectfully listen to each other and solve everyday problems and demonstrate what it means to truly commit to the marital relationship.

BUT, WHAT ABOUT *MY* HAPPINESS?

Certainly, no loving parent would intentionally cause their children emotional harm or stack the cards against them regarding future healthy intimate relationships and happiness. Still, generations of children have been tossed about and *their* emotional needs have taken a back seat to their parents' search for *happiness* or an elusive feeling of *being in love*. Wallerstein's findings should spur couples considering marriage with children to take a hard look at the *responsibilities of marriage with children*. Rather than taking an attitude of *We will cross that bridge when we come to it*, couples need to decide ahead of time whether leaving a family unit is an option when they *no longer feel love* for their partner. I believe consideration of children's present and future happiness should have at least equal weight in a decision involving divorce.

Wallerstein and others (2000) found that couples who stayed "unhappily" married, made parenting their number one priority. They write: "The notion that open conflict is the hallmark of unhappy marriages is simply not true. That children are aware of their parents' unhappiness and are themselves unhappy because of it is also not true. It depends on whether the parents are able with grace and without anger to make the sacrifice required to maintain the benefits of the marriage *for their children's sake*."(Italics provided.)

According to Dr. Wallerstein, we have created a new kind of society never before seen in human culture: *a culture of divorce.* One fourth (25%) of people today between the ages of 18 and 44 have parents who divorced at least once (most divorced persons remarry). Kids of divorce often suffer multiple losses as parents go through future lovers and at least one new spouse. In light of the often harsh consequences of the choice to divorce, we must ask ourselves if we are providing the best future for our children and ensuing generations.

You might want to reflect on the following:

- Do my children talk disrespectfully because that's the way I talk to my spouse?
- Do my children have difficulty concentrating in school partly because they are worried by the constant tension and bickering between my spouse and me?
- Am I willing to make changes in myself and my marriage for my children's welfare?

FAMILY HISTORIES MAY INTERTWINE: "The Daisy-Chain Effect"

Family histories can daisy-chain their way into the present. Despite our best intentions not to "do what our parents did," unless we are taught new skills and attitudes, we often repeat our parents' past behavior and mistakes. The way we related to our parents may influence, either positively or negatively, how we relate to our children. We may have, but not recognize, the same overly high standards our parents had for us. Or, perhaps we are quick to show anger when our children do not listen or move quickly enough. Maybe you shriek when your 3-year-old accidentally spills milk or slams the door too loudly.

It can be helpful to determine if childhood issues are negatively impacting your life. Counseling may bring these issues to light and provide an opportunity for you to understand and work through them. Notice especially if childhood issues show up in your anger diaries.

As a child, if you experienced distancing or a rejecting love by a parent you may find it difficult to form a close bond with your children. Past unconscious hurts remain with us until we identify and work through the traumas which caused those hurts. If a negative family pattern is contributing to your child's behavior/discipline problems, make a commitment to change that pattern. Ask yourself and reflect on the following questions:

- Is my child afraid to take risks because I am afraid to take risks?

- Am I yelling at my child the way my Dad/Mom yelled at me?
- Do I feel victimized by my strong-minded child because I feel victimized in general?
- Is it difficult for me to assert myself with my child because I was never encouraged to be assertive while I was growing up?

PARENTS' ANGER VIEWED THROUGH CHILDREN'S EYES

To a young child, a parent's anger outburst is not only terrifying but may trigger fears of abandonment. "You hate me" and "You wish I were dead" are common remarks from preschoolers after being screamed at by their parents. We often forget our young children depend on us for their survival. If, in their minds, we stop *liking* them, they fear they might die — emotionally and physically.

The irritation, disgust and rage we may express toward our children can be an emotional release for us. But to them it can feel like intense rejection and disapproval for who they are and what they do. Children develop their self-concept, self-esteem, view of themselves, and self-acceptance from parents. If they think or feel as if we do not like them, children may begin to hate themselves. *Research shows that children view themselves through our eyes.* Without parental approval and the feeling they are cherished and loved, children feel insecure and are more likely to seek approval from any source.

Many of you may have learned to avoid your angry parents. You may have been the *good kid,* anticipating what would make your parents mad and doing everything right to escape their verbal and, perhaps, physical wrath. Or, maybe those of you who were *strong-willed* somehow never learned to stuff your feelings and just obey. You felt compelled to fight back. As a result, you probably received a lot of verbal and physical punishment and may retain pent up anger.

Thinking Point: How can you make your child's experiences better?

The Good and The Bad and The Sometimes Ugly

Anger is an emotional reaction to a perceived provocation. Of all the emotions, anger is perhaps the most confusing. We tend to view anger as a negative emotion, yet it has a number of important adaptive functions. For instance, anger gives us added energy to react in self-defense when we are attacked physically, verbally, or emotionally.

We may experience anger when we see something we feel is unjust, unfair, frustrating or annoying. Anger transformed into commitment of purpose often gives us the stamina we need to complete a difficult task or to respond to danger. Once we have transformed anger into positive action, anger is a useful emotion. We can be motivated by anger to assertively correct an injustice. When you are assertive (not aggressive or passive), the feelings of others are taken into consideration as you clearly state what you need or want from the situation. When expressed assertively and respectfully, anger transformed into positive action can communicate that you feel strongly about an issue or your personal boundaries.

Still, anger is best known for its negative functions. If too intense, you may fail to think clearly and may behave impulsively. You may find yourself screeching and gesturing wildly when you see your 9-year-old playing instead of getting ready for school. At times, you may feel as if you are operating purely on emotions with no rational thought involved.

Remember:

- Unrestrained anger can give you a false sense of control.
- Intense, out of control anger can increase verbal and physical aggression by inciting others to defend themselves.
- Anger often is a defensive posture you exhibit when you feel afraid, hurt, or embarrassed.

Stuffing your anger could present a new set of problems:

- Repressed anger has been associated with an increase in hypertension, heart disease, ulcers, and other serious health concerns.
- Feeling as if you cannot express your anger may lead to feelings of helplessness and hopelessness often associated with depression.
- Both depressed thinking and angry thinking can come from and lead to distorted or incorrect thinking about ourselves, others, and the world.

Too, consider the negative or damaging effects of your anger outbursts which:

- Frighten your kids.
- Damage their self-esteem.
- Create negative feelings.
- Model out of control behavior to your kids.
- Prevent effective problem solving opportunities.
- Reinforce a bad habit of losing self-control.
- Are upsetting to other family members.
- Cause you extreme stress.

Thinking Point:

Through training, you will learn how to transform your anger-energy into positive action and to use it effectively — within safe boundaries.

*COGNITIVE-BEHAVIOR ANGER MODEL

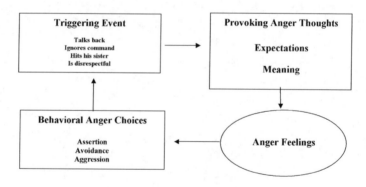

*adapted from Novaco (1977)

The Cognitive-Behavioral Anger Model was initially developed by Dr. Raymond Novaco (1977) and the following discussion is based on his work. This model illustrates the interactions between Triggering Events, Provoking Thoughts and Behavioral Factors which determine the feeling we call *anger*. For example:

(1) A ***triggering event*** occurs which is processed internally according to our expectations of how things *should be* and *what the event means to us.*

(2) *How we view the anger-provoking event* determines our level of anger, or whether we will become angry.

(3) We then *select a behavioral response to the situation,* perhaps by attacking verbally or physically, or withdrawing and retreating. Ideally, you would react assertively: (Remember: Behaving assertively means considering the other person's needs and feelings and stating clearly what you want from the situation.)

Finally, the cognitive-behavioral model of anger suggests that our response to the provocation influences how the other person will respond to us. This chain of interaction continues in reciprocal fashion and may escalate over time. Examining the four sections of the model will clarify the interactions.

Triggering Anger Events

1. **Frustration** is defined as: *A feeling of dissatisfaction often accompanied by anxiety or depression, resulting from unfulfilled needs or unresolved problems.* You may attempt to do something (clean, read, or work) and you are prevented or blocked from doing it. Or, you want to finish an interesting newspaper article and one by one your children ask for something, requiring you to stop and attend to their needs or wants. It is common to feel frustrated when you are in a hurry and get stuck in traffic or when your kids seem to dawdle in getting dressed. Frustration can envelop you when you expect or hope that something positive will happen and it doesn't: Your 12-year-old *promised* to have the kitchen clean for expected guests. You go to work or attend to other matters and when you return home, the kitchen is just as you left it.

2. **Annoyance** is defined as: *A disturbance or bothering in a way that displeases, troubles, or irritates.* You may be annoyed or irritated when something gets on your nerves such as excessive noise or behavior you find disturbing. Whining is often reported as a child behavior that produces the highest level of irritation in parents. Other annoyances could include a child accidentally ripping your favorite dress, or dropping a salad you just spent 45 minutes preparing. Your 10-year-old tapping his fingers on the table to a tune only he hears can also prove irksome.

3. **Abuse** can be defined as: *Treating in a harmful or injurious way; using insulting language in a harsh or coarse way; improper treatment.* When we experience either verbal (name-calling, cursing, speaking

sarcastically) or physical abuse (pushing, kicking, grabbing) we may react in anger.

4. **Unfairness** can be defined as: *Not conforming to standards of honesty or justice; improper; disproportionate.* Feeling as if you've been treated unfairly is a key link to an anger response. You might think: *It's not fair that I work so hard to keep the house clean and the kids just mess it up.* Thinking of an injustice (cultural cleansing, abused children) can incite feelings of anger. The positive side: You may be motivated to take action and make a significant change in the status quo.

Internal Anger Thoughts

1. **Expectation** is defined as: *An anticipation of an occurrence; the degree of probability that something will occur.* For example: *My kids are old enough to put their clothes away and not to leave clothes on the floor. I shouldn't have to remind him to do his homework. He knows better than to leave without telling me where he's going. You should have had your pajamas on by 8:00 p.m.!* Whenever your expectations are not met, you may become angry because things are not the way you thought they should be. When you feel a sense of unfairness and personalization, you may experience anger arising out of feelings of indignation and mistreatment.

Parents often take their children's behavior personally, as if their kids intentionally try to incite anger by their behavior. Mom recalls how 4-year-old Jason yells and slams toys around.

Mom thinks: *"He knew I just put the baby down. He is so selfish. He knows Aaron is sleeping!"*

Mom yells: *"I can't believe you're making so much noise! You know Aaron is sleeping!"*

Jason probably just wanted to have fun with his toy. Mom's negative attention — in the form of yelling — may be maintaining Jason's negative behavior.

I give him attention all day long, but every time I speak on the phone he interrupts me! This Mother believes that since she gave Jason attention all day, he shouldn't have to interrupt her phone calls. He should realize he has had enough attention. When this expectation is not met, Mother becomes angry. Her level of anger is partially determined by how strongly she feels Jason should have known not to interrupt, and her perception of the unfairness of his actions.

2. **Meaning** is defined as: *What is intended to be or actually is*

expressed or indicated; the purpose or significance of something. Mary's 5-year-old son was throwing a tantrum and talking disrespectfully to her when they were alone at home. She felt less anger than when he did the same thing in front of her in-laws. In terms of her child-rearing skills, Mary often feels negatively judged by her Mother-in-law. Mary is eager to demonstrate she is a good disciplinarian and has taught her son appropriate behavior.

Anger producing thoughts racing through Mary's mind when Grandma's eyes show disapproval may include: *Oh, why did you have to say that in front of her? You are showing her what a lousy parent I am. He is just acting up to embarrass me after all I did for him today! I know he's going to go on and on!*

Mary feels that her self-esteem is on the line. Her thoughts reveal she is taking her son's tantrum and disrespectful words personally. She feels out of control, embarrassed, and negatively judged by Grandma. Mary also feels as if her son is not being "fair" to her since she did so much for him today. Again, these thoughts not only reflect the expectations and meaning her son's behavior has for her, but illustrate how her thoughts cause her anger to escalate.

When you are rushed and on a tight schedule, anger is more likely to occur because: Your level of patience is down and your level of frustration is up.

In Summary:

The way you *think* about a situation — not the situation itself, or the person(s) involved — causes and determines the extent of your anger. Our angry thoughts lead to the emotional feeling we call *anger*.

Behavioral Anger Factors

Once we feel anger, we may react in one of three ways:
- **Avoidance,**
- **Aggression,** or
- **Assertion.**

Referring to the Anger Model, note that your reaction will influence how others react to you. Their reactions then influence what you will say and do next (external, internal, or behavioral).

1. **Avoidance** is defined as: *Keeping away from; preventing from happening; abstaining from or shunning.* One may want to avoid all

confrontations. Avoidance does not make the problem go away, but serves as a coping mechanism some people use when they cannot deal with the problem properly.

2. **Aggression** is defined as: *Any offensive action, attack, or procedure; hostility toward or attack upon another, whether overt, verbal, or by gesture.* Spanking, slapping, or verbally abusing a child only demonstrates to the child what should not occur. When a child sees a parent's angry response, the child will probably react in the same way in future. This promotes negative behaviors and no positive behaviors are reinforced or demonstrated.

3. **Assertion** is defined as: *A positive statement or declaration, often without support or reason; an allegation.* Ideally, we assert ourselves saying respectfully and directly what we need and expect from the other person. We define exactly what we want and state (not ask) what is expected.

ANGER: ALWAYS TROLLING FOR "HITCH-HIKERS"

As you examine your thoughts, actions, and reactions in stressful situations, you can see more clearly that: "Anger Never Travels Alone" — it *requires* a traveling companion. Anger outbursts are often triggered by these "hitchers:"

- Feelings of physical tenseness (usually a chronic state of tension), irritation, moodiness, or pressure due to lack of time, causing you to overreact.
- Perpetual moodiness or pessimism (seeing a glass as half empty), making you feel things are not going to get better no matter how hard you try.
- Children's non-stop misbehavior (noise or constant demands), causing you to lash out verbally when you are pushed beyond your emotional and physical limits.

Learning to recognize what sets your anger in motion:
- Helps you to control your reactions to external or internal factors.
- Helps you to cultivate behavioral reactions that are positive and constructive.

Let all bitterness, wrath, anger, clamor . . . be put away from you . . . And be kind to one another, tenderhearted, forgiving one another . . . . (Ephesians 4: 31-32)

CHAPTER 4

"A NEW WAY TO VIEW ABCs"

FOLLOWING ARE ABCs THAT DIFFER FROM THE STANDARD "A" is for Apple; "B" is for Boy; and "C" is for Cat. *They form the building blocks of your behavior change program. This will be your working formula for determining why your child behaves the way he does.* You will continue to use this formula whenever *future* problem behaviors occur.

THE ABCs OF BEHAVIORAL CHANGE

This acronym stands for:
- Antecedents
- Behavior
- Consequences

A: THE ANTECEDENTS

Antecedents take place prior to a behavior and influence the behavior that follows. Identifying the antecedents will provide clues as to why a particular behavior is occurring. **Antecedents are anything that influence your child's behavior**, including the following:

- Child's temperament.
- Impact of TV programs, video games, and movies.
- Family environment.
- Health and mood of the parent and child.
- Time of day and day of week.
- People involved in the interactions (parent, brother, sister, neighbor, or relative).
- Behavior that came right before your child's behavior (brother hit child and child hit back).
- Sarcastic remark made by parent; child retorted with a similar remark.

You might address the following questions:

1. Is the child acting aggressively, in part, because you and your spouse speak aggressively to one another?

2. Do you appear to be attacking, hostile, or irritated in your facial expression or tone of voice? (If so, your child is likely to reply with a similar negative tone or retort.)

3. Are the children teasing each other because they subconsciously feel there is not enough love, comfort, time, or attention from their two-working-parents to go around?

4. Are they talking sarcastically to each other because the family value of *respect for others* is not taught and modeled daily?

5. Does your marital relationship affect your child's problem behavior?

The ***type of command*** you give to your child is another important ***antecedent*** that will determine whether or not your child obeys.

COMMANDS: "I Know I'm Talking . . . I Hear Me!"

Commands are antecedents that have a high degree of influence on your child's behavior. Clinical research shows that the *type* command given a child directly affects the subsequent behavior. **Are you the only one *listening* to yourself?** Learn to use methods of communication that insure your *children* are listening to you. When instructions are given as *requests,* the implication is: *When and if you have time, or feel so inclined.* They are not *commands.*

Many parents, Mothers especially, have difficulty giving clear, direct commands. Perhaps, due to cultural training, childhood conditioning or temperament, you do not feel comfortable giving commands to your children. Maybe you have difficulty being direct with people in general. When you strengthen your skills in this area, you will feel more comfortable and confident when telling your child what you expect. If needed, assertion training classes are available.

To be an effective disciplinarian, you must communicate to your children that you mean what you say and will follow-through with consequences. Together with verbal expression, communicate with your tone of voice and physical presence, making sure your child complies. ***To increase your credibility***, be consistent at following through with consequences so your children know: *You mean what you say.*

Once you have mastered the ACP steps, you will feel less intimidated and out of control when your kids shout back in protest. You will be less reluctant to give a straightforward command, fearing the children will erupt into verbal and physical fallout. Instead, you will take a deep breath, relax your muscles and proceed to hold your ground confidently. You will know *exactly* what you need to do and will stand firm knowing that: *You hold the keys to all the privileges your kids desire!*

Learn To Give Effective Instructions And Commands

Effective Commands **are:**
- clear,
- direct, and
- simple.

Ineffective Commands are:
- unclear,
- indirect,
- vague,
- complicated,
- consist of chains of commands, or
- issued as questions.

(More discussion will follow about how to give effective commands.)

B: THE BEHAVIOR

DEFINE AND LABEL THE BEHAVIOR SPECIFICALLY

Our tendency is to generalize (often negatively) in describing the behavior of others. At times we apply global terms to our children's behavior. These terms can become labels which describe the *whole* person and may shame the child in some way. For example, you might refer to your child as being *lazy*, or a *manipulator, trouble maker*, or *the terminator*, etc.

This approach to viewing your child can cause you to attend more to their negative behaviors that provide *evidence* the child is *difficult, bratty*, etc. You may focus only on examples of behavior which support your negative view of your child. For instance, every sassy word reinforces your view of your child as a *disrespectful brat*. As a result you may overlook your child's positive behaviors such as performing assigned chores and picking up toys when told to do so.

It is important to specifically define your child's behavior in terms that allow you to keep track. Instead of "My kid is the terminator," define his negative behaviors: "He hits," or "spits," or "runs away when called." These behaviors can be counted. Defining the behavior (versus the person) allows parents to label, list and notice both negative and positive behaviors. Note especially if your *terminator* exhibits positive behaviors: getting dressed without parental coaching every step of the way or working for long periods of time on a project, etc.

In Summary: It is important to specifically define and label your kid's behaviors for the following reasons:

- You will be more objective in noticing both negative and positive behaviors.
- You can count how often the behaviors occur initially and review the results again after a few weeks into the ACP program for comparison.
- You will teach your child that though he exhibits inappropriate behaviors (hitting), he is still lovable.
- You will realize that targeted behaviors are more easily changed than global labels.
- Your child will not get stuck in a role (*the difficult one*), but will realize they can learn new positive behaviors.

Your child will feel more hopeful and develop greater self-esteem. To illustrate: We can count the number of times *dishes are taken to the sink* easier than trying to tally *being a lazy pig*. Behaviors represent just one of many parts of the whole person and can be changed. In contrast, labels suggest indelible traits that often stick with the child. Below is an exercise to practice specifically labeling your child's behaviors.

Take time to practice specifically defining behaviors you want to change, for example:

Say This:	**Instead Of:**
"I like how you took your dishes to the sink."	"You're so nice."
"You were hitting your brother. Keep your hands to yourself. You lose a point and now go to time-out for 10 minutes."	"What a brat."
"When I see your clothes in the hamper, I'll put a quarter in your bank."	"What a slob!"

Think of behaviors you want maintained and increased; then think of behaviors you want decreased or eliminated.

Example:

Behaviors to Maintain and/or Increase:	**Specifically Defined As:**
1. Kindness	1. Encourages others; shares
2. Responsibility	2. Remembers to bring lunch box home. Writes down and completes homework assignments
3. Obedience	3. Begins what he is told to do within 10 seconds
4. Neatness	4. Puts clothes and toys in proper places Writes carefully on paper

Behaviors to Decrease:	**Specifically Defined As:**
1. Rudeness	1. Talks loudly, sticks tongue out, and interrupts
2. Aggressiveness	2. Hitting, yelling, spitting, and pushing
3. Disobedience	3. Not coming when called Does opposite of what is told
4. Disrespectful talk	4. Sarcastic, flippant tone ("Yeah right, duh!")

C: THE CONSEQUENCES

The consequence following a behavior is the most *critical* component of the ABC formula. The consequence determines whether the positive or negative behavior increases or decreases. *If the specific behavior increases over time then, by definition, the consequence is a reinforcer.* A reinforcer is *any* event that follows a behavior and **increases** the likelihood that the behavior will recur. *If a consequence follows a behavior and the behavior decreases over time, then it* is a *punisher.*

Remember, *a reinforcer is* any *event which follows a behavior and increases the likelihood that the behavior will recur.* Therefore, reinforcers can be either positive *or* negative parent responses.

NEGATIVE ATTENTION

Negative attention could be described as a universal parent's weakness. Parents often unknowingly reinforce and maintain and/ or increase obnoxious, irritating negative behaviors they strive to eliminate. Children will do *everything* they can to insure a steady flow of the verbal and physical reinforcement we call *love*. If parents do not provide positive reinforcements, a child will settle for negative attention. To a child, negative attention (parents yelling and scolding) is better than no attention. Children would rather be yelled at than ignored. They will increase their negative behavior if that's the only connection with their parents or caregivers.

Negative attention is the use of gestures, commands, etc., meant to reduce a behavior, but which generally cause an increase in that behavior. Examples include parents yelling at the child or giving disapproving looks, but failing to provide a back-up consequence for the behavior.

Consider the Following Examples:

1. The child accidentally spilled milk:

Parent rolls eyes upward in exasperation or disgust saying, "I can't believe you did that!" No other consequence is given.

2. The child pushes his brother to shove him aside.

Parent: "Hey, stop that! That's no way to treat your brother! I don't know how you could do such a thing!" No other consequence is given.

3. Two kids are verbally fighting:

Parent: "I get so sick and tired of hearing you two argue! Why do you have to turn something fun into an argument?" No other consequence is given.

4. The child is swinging a wooden bat around near a window:

Parent: "Put that down!"

Child: Ignores parent, continues swinging bat.

Parent: Frowning and obviously irritated, grabs the bat and yells, "Can't you hear? What's wrong with you, anyway?" No other consequence is given.

5. The child puts his green beans into his glass of milk:

Parent: "How many times have I told you not to do that? You're acting like a 2-year-old! Why can't you just sit down at the table to eat without messing around? I really get tired of correcting you!" No other consequence is given.

These parents are providing a lot of attention — although it is negative — following undesirable behaviors. Again, any form of attention following a behavior will increase the chance that the behavior will recur. Additionally, the parents are modeling negative behavior (loss of self-control, name calling, verbally attacking child).

In the examples above, no effective consequence was provided. Ideally, the minor negative behaviors are ignored and when appropriate behaviors occur, they are praised. For more serious behaviors, the behavior is described and a consequence is given calmly.

Consider the following:

Child is picking his nose. Ignore the nose picking, hand the child a tissue and praise immediately when the child uses a tissue. For example, say as you hand child a tissue, "It looks like you need a tissue. Remember, we use a tissue for our boogies." The parent praises the child as he uses a tissue and ignores any protest that he does not want to. The parent can also use modeling. For example, the parent talks aloud so the child can hear and see how she uses a tissue for her boogies. She may comment, "Mommy uses a tissue when her boogies bother her."

When negative behavior occurs, the parent calmly describes the behavior and the broken rule: "I expect you to use your words not your hands. You lost a point. Go to time-out." (Parent sets timer.) These parental responses are in contrast to: "Stop waving the stick around, you can hurt someone. How old are you going to be before you learn it?" These types of negative responses do not teach the child an *alternate* behavior. In addition, the child is not given an opportunity to *practice* the correct response.

PUNISHERS

Consequences that follow a behavior and decrease the likelihood the behavior will happen again are called *punishers*. ACP primarily focuses on the use of ***time-out*** and ***losing/earning privileges*** to decrease negative behavior. Time-out is a mild form of punishment, where all reinforcement is removed. Although brief, time-out is usually unpleasant for the child. Their activity is interrupted and the time spent is boring. Following negative behaviors with time-out and/or revoking privileges likely will cause the behaviors to occur less often.

As discussed below, spanking your child is not an effective option for punishment. Spanking, by definition, is the application of physical pain. When spanking follows a negative behavior, the behavior may decrease over time. However, to be effective, spanking must hurt and have "shock value." To achieve this, spanking must be administered infrequently. Spanking a child every day may lead to a tolerance of the pain level needed to achieve the initial effect. The parent will then have to spank harder and harder, putting the child at risk for abuse.

Spanking **is not a preferred method of discipline and is discouraged by most child behavior professionals.**

WHAT YOU TEACH YOUR CHILD/ WHAT YOUR CHILD TEACHES YOU

The following comments are ones frequently voiced by parents at my seminars:

> *"Why won't my child obey the first time I ask?"*
> *"Why do I have to keep repeating myself until I lose all patience and start yelling?"*
> *"I never thought there would be so much yelling and crying in my family."*
> *"All I hear all day is, 'MOM, he's bugging me!'"*

CHAIN OF NEGATIVE INTERACTION

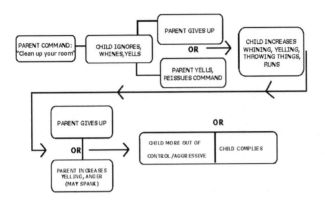

*adapted from Patterson (1976) as cited in Forehand & McMahon (1981).
Adapted here with permission from Guilford Press.

With training and understanding, parents can turn a negative family environment into a more cooperative and loving one. Further:

- You will travel a calmer path as you learn there are underlying reasons why so many families drift into negative ways of interrelating.
- You will see that it is necessary to identify and address these underlying reasons.
- You will learn why parents resort to yelling to get their children to obey, and how children learn to punish their parents to get what they want.

Dr. Gerald Patterson developed what he calls the *Coercion Hypothesis* to explain how parents and children develop and maintain each other's behaviors. Patterson (1976, as cited in Forehand & McMahon, 1981) suggests that infants and young children exhibit behaviors such as whining, crying, and tantrums as an appropriate developmental way to get their needs met. Ideally, with age and training, infants and toddlers develop the verbal, cognitive and social ability to communicate in a more appropriate manner. Often, parents inadvertently continue to reinforce and respond to their child's *infant* ways of getting what they want (whining, protesting relentlessly).

Patterson states that: **Negative reinforcement** is the primary mechanism in the development and maintenance of negative child and parent behaviors. Negative reinforcement occurs when a punishing event or behavior is turned off. Removing a painful or negative event following a behavior increases the likelihood that the behavior will occur more often. Following is an example of negative reinforcement:

- Mother asks Dylan to clean up his room.
- Dylan starts to whine and yell.
- Mother repeats her command for Dylan to clean up his room.
- Dylan increases his whining and yelling.
- Mother yells at Dylan to clean up his room.
- Dylan resists and continues his whining and yelling.
- Mother gives in and withdraws her command ("Okay, forget it. I'll do it myself!").

Mother's command to clean up was punishing to Dylan. Dylan's whining and yelling was punishing to Mother. Negative reinforcement occurs when you remove a punishing event following a behavior. In the example above, Mother removed her command following Dylan's continued whining and yelling. Dylan stopped whining and yelling after Mother withdrew her request. Following a behavior with negative (or positive) reinforcement increases the likelihood that the behavior will occur more frequently. Dylan's whining and yelling were negatively reinforced and will occur with greater frequency when Mother gives future commands.

Mother giving in to Dylan's protest was also negatively reinforced when Dylan removed his whining and protesting. Dylan may eventually train Mother (via negative reinforcement) to be reluctant to give any commands. Most parents have experienced that this negative chain of interaction continues as both parent and child escalate the intensity of their negative behaviors.

Several things are important to note about the chain of negative interactions:

- First, notice the length of the chain: The longer the chain, the longer both parent and child practice negative behavior (verbally attacking, screaming, whining, and yelling).
- Second, the longer the chain, the more likely the negative behaviors escalate in intensity.
- When Mother first gave the command, she was relatively calm, firm and in control. However, when she repeats herself, she becomes irritated and speaks louder.
- By the third repeated command, Mother becomes visibly agitated, is yelling and ready to spank. In similar fashion, Dylan escalated the intensity and ferocity of his behavior.

Research shows that children are at greater risk for abuse as the chain lengthens. If Mother withdraws her command at a later point in the chain, she will reinforce child behavior that is more intense and negative than earlier child responses. Mother can expect as these interactions are repeated daily, that Dylan will respond with a louder, more aggressive behavior earlier in the chain.

In future when Mother issues her first command to clean up, Dylan is more likely to shout loudly, "No!" as he throws a toy in her direction. He has learned (by negative reinforcement) that Mother is more likely to "give up" when he escalates his negative behavior. Similarly, if the child complies after Mother escalates *her* negative behavior (screaming, threatening, spanking); Mother is more likely to use intensive negative behavior sooner in the chain. She is being trained (by negative reinforcement) that yelling and screaming works, at least in the short term. It usually gets rapid compliance; but parents soon will tire of paying the price. Mother is also modeling aggressive, out of control behavior to Dylan, increasing the likelihood he will show similar behavior in future.

This process has been termed the **negative reinforcement trap.** *The goal is to keep the discipline interaction chain short:*

- A firm command is given once. Do not repeat yourself.
- If the command is obeyed, praise is given immediately.
- If the command is disobeyed, a mild punishment (time-out or loss of privilege) is given in a calm manner.

In this way, Mother models self-control and her child's self-esteem remains intact as he learns what behaviors are expected of him.

PUNISHMENT ALONE DOESN'T WORK — There's a Reason

As stated previously, many parents come to my ACP seminars hoping to learn the most effective way to punish their children's negative behavior. They say, "I've tried time-out, spanking, scolding, taking things away; nothing works! I still can't get Karina to do what I ask the first time." Parents typically rely on punishment because it is a quick and relatively easy way to stop the negative behavior. Unfortunately, they also are modeling reliance on easy, violent solutions to problems. Punishment may take less time than trying to understand why the problem is occurring. But **punishment alone does not focus on** *preventing* **the problem or bringing about the** *opposite, appropriate behavior* **using positive means.** Behavioral research shows it is most effective for parents to *first use positive techniques before using more negative forms of discipline*

Remember: Discipline means *teaching and instructing.* Relying solely on punishment is not the best way to *teach* children to obey. Parents who rely primarily on punishment to teach their children how to behave eventually realize they do so at a great cost. Hearing mostly negative comments daily, children quickly build resentment toward their parents and tune out, often reducing and stifling positive feelings toward their parents. Most children hear negative evaluations each day from authority figures at the approximate rate of 6:1 (**negative to positive**). This is not the best way to *teach* children new behaviors or build their self-esteem. Set a goal to turn that ratio around to 8:1 (**positive to negative**).

In the book, *The Noncompliant Child,* Drs. Forehand & McMahon emphasize **using punishment only tells children** *what not to do.* For example, using a verbal reprimand like, "Don't hit," "Don't talk sarcastically," "Don't whine!" or "Stop fighting!" may temporarily stop or decrease the frequency of negative behaviors. But, only punishing negative behavior does not increase the opposite positive behavior. (See A in the following chart). **You must teach your child** *what behaviors to do* **instead.** (See B in the following chart). For example, say "Use your words not your hands," "Talk with respect," "Speak clearly," "Say what you want in a big girl/boy voice," "I expect you to try and resolve your differences." To build these new behaviors:

Children need guidance via role-play with parents, consistent, frequent attention, praise, and positive reinforcement daily.

Frequency Of Behavior Chart

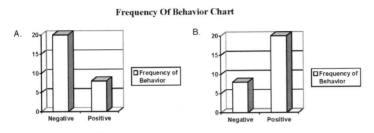

(*adapted from Forehand & McMahan (1981) with permission from Guilford Press)

Conversely, if parents focus on increasing their child's positive behaviors by positive praise and attention, the opposite negative behaviors *will* decrease in frequency. A child who is praised when he *speaks clearly* will learn to speak clearly more often, and *whine* less often. Punishing *whining* will *not* increase *speaking clearly* unless the child is specifically taught to do so (by positive praise, attention and practice through role-play).

Teaching a 3-year-old to ask for something with clear words (by immediate, continuous positive praise, attention, and modeling) will increase the number of times she asks with clear words instead of whining. Using only punishment (time-out, spanking, or privilege loss) will not guarantee the child will learn the proper way to ask for a turn playing with a toy, waiting for a turn, and so on. In fact, research shows that frequent reliance on punishment increases aggressiveness in kids.

To Summarize: Scolding or punishing your child when they display negative behavior may temporarily stop the behavior (whining). But, if the child has not also practiced and received reinforcement for expressing himself in a more appropriate way (speaking clearly), the negative behavior will return or some other negative behavior may take its place. As you have learned, scolding may be a form of reinforcement that causes negative behavior to increase over time. Using positive methods to increase desired behavior is the best way to teach your child, to build respectful, loving relationships, and preserve your child's self-esteem.

Thought Points:

- Punishing a negative behavior (whining) does not teach a child what to do instead.
- Praising the opposite positive behavior (speaking clearly) will result in a decrease in the negative behavior (whining).
- As the child increases their appropriate behavior (asking with words), they are less likely to perform the opposite negative behavior (grabbing).

SPANKING: Negative Effects of Physical Punishment

Many of our parents relied primarily on physical punishment to teach us to "behave." As noted earlier, focusing primarily on punishing negative behavior does not insure the child will learn the opposite positive behavior. Reliance primarily on physical punishment may have both short and long term negative consequences.

Unless a parent administers a spanking in a calm, planned manner, the child may be at risk for physical abuse. An angry, frustrated and out of control parent giving a spanking is starting out on a rush of adrenaline. Often the spanking doesn't stop until the parent's emotional release is over or they become physically exhausted. There is a danger that a young child may be unintentionally hurt.

Though the result falls short of physical abuse, both parents and children may have intense emotional reactions to physical discipline. Parents often feel guilty about the pain they inflict and feel angry at the child as the residue of the physical confrontation lingers. And, parents may experience remorse after realizing they have over-spanked in reaction to pent-up feelings or frustration. Extensive punishment also sets up "escape/avoidance" behaviors. A child may resort to lying to avoid physical punishment or attempt to avoid contact with the parent altogether. For example:

A Mother brought her 5-year-old son in for therapy. She described him as being a shy, reserved child. His father had disciplined him with a spanking on several occasions. The 5-year-old became so fearful and obsessive about the possibility of getting spanked that he questioned the possible consequence of each minor infraction. Thus, frequent physical punishment may result in other unwanted behaviors (increased fear, obsessing, avoidance).

Physical punishment is *not* suggested and is not effective as a discipline measure because:

- Technically, to be effective, physical punishment must hurt and have "shock value."
- Daily use of physical punishment allows the child to build up a tolerance for the pain level administered.
- Physical punishment then loses effectiveness in influencing long-lasting behavior change.
- More severe physical punishment, administered more frequently, is required to achieve the same result.

Overuse of physical punishment may provide an aggressive model for the child. Used exclusively for discipline, such punishment may teach a child to resort to physical or violent means to solve their problems or as a reaction to the mistakes others make. Children show high rates of aggressive behavior when parents are verbally or physically aggressive.

Physical punishment appears to achieve quick, short term results, reinforcing parents to use it again. However, after a short time the misbehavior recurs. For example: Spanking children for fighting may temporarily stop the brawl, but within 30 minutes Mary calls Jason a name and the fight resumes.

An unwanted side effect of overuse of physical punishment is: It may cause parents to lose their value as a positive reinforcer. Associating yourself with frequent physical punishment and bouts of anger may cause your children to dislike you or not desire to please you. It is not uncommon for children to try and avoid this type parent.

"A"ntecedents Continued: INEFFECTIVE COMMANDS

Parents who give their children vague or complicated commands discover their children often balk at complying. Parental commands are immediately analyzed by children (from a child's point of view, based on past experience) to determine whether or not their parents will enforce what they say.

In their book, *The Noncompliant Child*, Drs. Forehand & McMahan identified four main types of *ineffective commands*:

- **Question Commands**
- **Let's Commands**
- **Chain Commands**
- **Vague Commands**

1. Question Commands

Question commands are actually questions and not direct commands *to do* or *not do* something. When children detect a tentativeness or hesitation in the request, they are less likely to obey.

For example, change "How about we clean up?" to "Come and pick up your toys." Change "Don't you think it's getting late and you should go to bed?" to "It is 7:30 p.m. and bedtime will be in 15 minutes." Change "Don't you think your room's a mess?" to "Make your bed and put the dirty clothes in the hamper by 10:00 a.m."

2. Let's Commands

The child interprets this type command as a *suggestion* rather than instructions that they exhibit a specified behavior. Also implied is that you are going to help or participate in the activity (which is okay if you plan to do so).

For example, change "Let's put away these toys," to "Jamie, when the timer dings, it will be time for you to put away your toys." Change "Let's be quieter," to "Jamie, talk softer." Change "Let's be nice to each other," to "I expect you to talk with respect to your friends."

3. Chain Commands

Stringing several commands together makes it difficult for children to remember and perform each task. Preschoolers and children with Attention Deficit Hyperactivity Disorder (ADHD), in particular, are less likely to become confused if they are issued single commands. Always provide the subsequent consequence before you give the next command. A long list of commands can overwhelm any child.

For example, Dad says to 4-year-old Todd, "I want you to brush your teeth, wash your face and hands, and clean up that mess in the bathroom." To 6-year-old Kylie, he says, "Go in and clean your room, finish your math page, and do something with your hair!" Issue each command separately. Then, monitor, encourage and praise your children as they begin and end each task; then go to the next command.

For example, "John, come in and brush your teeth." (Followed by, "I like how you came so quickly!") "Now, I'm going to wash your face. Close your eyes." (Followed by, "Thanks for helping me.") "It's time for lunch, go and sit at the table." (Followed by, "You're moving so quickly; I like that.") Staying with your child and responding immediately to either their obedience or noncompliance helps them stay on task and learn new behaviors much quicker.

4. Vague Commands

Children are more likely to comply in response to clear, specific commands. We get upset if our children are unable to *read between the lines*, though we may have issued instructions that were too general and, therefore, confusing. Noncompliance is more likely when vague commands are given and such commands frequently cause misunderstandings between parent and child.

To prevent a misunderstanding, describe specifically what behavior you expect. For teenagers, put the expectations in writing and have them sign a simple contract. For instance: "John agrees to be home tonight by 10:00 p.m. If he is more than 15 minutes late, he will pay a $15 penalty and will not be allowed to go out next weekend." Consider the examples below:

Say This:	Instead Of:
"Two hands on the bar when climbing."	"Be careful."
"I expect you to wear a helmet and kneepads when you skateboard."	"Don't get hurt."
"Look both ways before you cross the street."	"Watch where you walk."
"I want you home by 10:30 p.m. Sign here so there will be no misunderstanding."	"Come home early."

Another *ineffective command* type is: Pleading Commands: "Please clean and straighten up; I don't want Grandma to think we have a messy house!" Children are not adults and they do not think like adults. They are not always motivated by altruistic behavior like an adult might be. For that reason, tell your child specifically what you want or expect them to do and provide an appropriate consequence.

Do not expect kids to do what you want out of the kindness of their hearts. Give a child a rationale as to why you want them to do something: State the reason first and always end with the command.

For example, "Grandma is coming for a visit and I want the house to look nice. Go in and make your bed and put your clothes in the dresser." "The weather person said there will be rain today. Put your umbrella in your backpack."

"A"ntecedents Continued: EFFECTIVE COMMANDS

Knowing how to give effective commands to your child will prevent miscommunication and will help your child to learn exactly what behaviors are expected. You just learned what *not to do*; now learn how to give effective parental commands by using the five suggestions below (McMahon & Forehand, 1981):

1. Be Where Your Child is At

Be physically close to your child when you give a command. Parents often yell from one room to another, say, the kitchen to the den, to give instructions. Children may interpret this behavior as the parent not really being serious about what they are asking. Kids size-up whether or not you have the energy and motivation at any given moment to follow-through with your commands.

When you are in close proximity to the child, you can observe whether your child complies with your command and you can respond accordingly. Also, your presence conveys the impression that you mean what you say: You're watching whether they comply and you're ready to follow-through with a consequence if necessary. Further, you are modeling respectful behavior by not yelling. Speak politely — but firmly.

2. Make Eye Contact With Your Child

Good eye contact also requires close proximity and conveys that you feel confident and are serious about what you are asking. Eye contact also insures that your children are listening and understand what you are saying. Being in close proximity and making eye contact with your child also models respect. **Always speak and behave respectfully with your children, just as you do with adults.**

3. Be Specific, Direct and Issue One Command at a Time

Specifically label the behavior you want so both you and your child are clear about what you expect. For example say, "I'm setting the timer for five minutes and I expect you to put away your blocks before the bell dings." "You were not excused, come back to the table." (Rationale stated first.) "Don't be late coming home. If you are later than five minutes, you will not go out next weekend. Be home by 8:30 p.m. tonight." "That was a disrespectful remark. Come sit on the chair for five minutes."

4. Use Body and Hand Gestures to Further Explain and Emphasize Your Command

Take care to not overwhelm or frighten your child with quick, forceful moves. Model self-control as you practice breathing and relaxation techniques to relax your mind and your body muscles. You can then communicate physically what you want: You can point in the direction of the chair you want your child to go to as you say, "You may not hit your sister. Go to the chair for six minutes."

5. Speak In a Serious Voice While Reflecting Self-Control

Speaking in a firm voice without sounding overly irritated or angry may be challenging. The goal is to communicate that you mean what you say and you will back it up. Unfortunately, our irritation and frustration are often heard in our voice. The result: We unintentionally provide negative attention following the child's behavior.

Remember: Negative attention reinforces and increases the frequency of your child's negative behavior.

Practice acquiring a firm but not excessively angry voice. Do this by thinking about a discipline situation and then speaking into a tape recorder. When you play back the tape, determine how specific and firm you were. Did you *overdo* it? Practice until you feel you have it right.

6. Give a Command Only if You Have the Energy and Ability to Back It Up

This requires that you be honest with yourself and admit when you're too emotionally or physically tired to follow-through with a command.

Remember: It is better not to give the command, rather than to give it and back down.

USE "DO" RATHER THAN "DON'T" COMMANDS

Say This:	Instead Of:
"Walk slowly."	"Don't run!"
"Talk with respect."	"Don't talk disrespectfully."
"Take the plate to the sink first, and return for the glass."	"Don't put the glass on the plate; it might fall."
"Use two hands when riding your bike."	"Don't take your hands off the handlebars; you might fall."
"I expect you to sit quietly and show self-control."	"Don't wiggle and make a lot of noise."
"Put away a game when you finish playing with it, before choosing another. Put away all the games when you've finished playing."	"Don't pull all the games out and don't make a big mess!"

Remember: *Do* commands tell the child what *To Do* instead of only what *Not to Do*. This makes it easier for the child to learn the positive behavior you desire. Verbalizing a positive behavior you want, instead of a negative behavior you anticipate, communicates encouragement rather than negativity. Let your child experience that you believe in them; that you know they can behave appropriately.

On a simple chart, note the type of commands you give this week. Next week change charts and notice your positive changes!

As stated earlier, our kids hear much more negative than positive evaluation each day. Stating your commands and requests in a positive light can also help increase the ratio of positive to negative comments kids hear. This will help to build, rather than tear down, their self-esteem.

FOCUSING ON THE "A"NTECEDENTS: "AN OUNCE OF PREVENTION . . ."

To stave off having to use *a pound of cure*: Recall that feedback regarding your children's daily behavior and choices is overwhelmingly negative. The lesser amount of positive relative to negative comments made to a child often has an adverse impact on children's self-esteem, especially if they frequently misbehave. To reduce the number of times discipline encounters could escalate into a negative interchange, it is important to prevent the misbehavior from occurring, if possible.

It's Seldom, "No!" — It's Usually, "No, No!"

As a child matures, more is expected of them in terms of internal control and staying away from items and areas off-limits. Until then, making simple changes in your house can create a more pleasant family atmosphere by reducing the number of "No's" you say to your toddler.

For example:

- Put plug covers on electrical outlets.
- Remove valued objects from lower shelves and tables.
- Put tape over TV and stereo knobs (to make touching them less desirable).
- Try to limit the number of areas and objects that are off-limits (TV dials, VCR buttons).
- Make your house as conducive for exploration and freedom as possible.
- Put locks on cupboards and closets you don't want your child to access.
- Secure important papers and other items to avoid a negative reaction if a young child finds and ruins them.
- You can put up door-gates to areas off-limits to the toddler.

Structuring a specific play area and choosing certain types of toys to be played with can act to rein in overly active preschoolers. Stay close to your toddlers, especially when they are engaged in group play. You need to carefully monitor their interactions and intervene to deflect possible negative behavior.

Observe and learn how long your preschooler and their playmates can play together before negative interchanges occur. If they are in pursuit of another child and raise a toy to throw or to hit with, you can quickly but gently take the toy and say, "We use our words, not our hands when we are angry."

In general, keep preschoolers' play periods with friends short: about 30-50 minutes. The goal is to have the session end on a positive note, before the children have an opportunity to initiate and "practice" peer reinforced negative behaviors. When preschoolers cry in reaction to a hit, the hitter is reinforced. Remember to speak to your young toddler in "positive/do" words; continually instructing them in "what to do" versus "what not to do" ("Walk slowly." "Talk with respect." "Use two hands when you drink your milk.").

Communicate Pre-Established Rules

Before each major daily activity begins (mealtime, play time, nap time), remind your child of the relevant rules and what they can expect to happen. Recite the rules verbally and/or use pictures in appropriate areas. In the bathroom, you can illustrate putting clothes in the hamper and placing the towel on the rack. At the table, you can picture feet on floor, one hand on lap. Show that eating and drinking occur only at the kitchen table or other *specifically designated places*. You can draw pictures to illustrate the rules depicting the examples below:

- Walk down hallway.
- We eat and drink only at the kitchen table or other *specifically designated places*.
- We take our dishes to the sink or dishwasher.

You might establish the rule that: When two or more kids want the same toy, turns will be taken by setting the timer for 10 minutes. When the timer dings, another person gets a turn. This method can serve to reassure each child they will not have to resort to physical persuasion or be tormented by the other children to be included. Have a timer available as an option when normal, spontaneous negotiation between children appears to break down. Using a timer to indicate how long a child has to dress, eat, finish homework, etc., also eliminates negative nagging and name calling by parents ("Why are you so lazy?").

State your expectations and the consequences ahead of time: "You can go out and play only if you finish your homework before the bell dings in 20 minutes." Then, your child clearly understands beforehand what is expected and the outcomes of the choices they make. Also, follow-through with the consequences: If the bell dings and homework is not done, do not allow them to go out and play.

Often, parents react negatively when their children do not do what parents *expect* they should do without being asked. If you delineate ahead of time what your behavioral expectations are and the subsequent consequences the child can expect, negative parent-child interaction can sometimes be avoided. Clear and specific commands will prevent misunderstandings and increase the likelihood that children will comply, thereby avoiding a negative punishment situation. (Example: "When you are finished with your snack, put your dishes in the dishwasher.")

To Preserve Your Child's Ego: Offer Choices

Be sensitive to your child's pride: Try not to *corner* them so they respond defensively with a "No!" reaction. Offer as many choices and options as possible. For example, if your headstrong 3-year-old refuses to go sit on the usual time-out chair, you might say, "Which chair are you going to sit on, the pink or the blue?" This allows them to feel as if they have some freedom in the situation and may block a quickly escalating negative confrontation. This is not to suggest they always have a choice of time-out locations. But, there are times when your child feels especially indignant and strong-willed about a situation. Try to work with him as you continue to focus on the desired outcome (going to time-out).

If you struggle with your child over what clothes they should wear, decide if this is an area that warrants a daily negative struggle. Such battles often set the tone for future altercations the remainder of the day. One suggestion: Have specific categories of acceptable clothes and let your child make choices. Have a rule that they may choose from most approved categories of clothes for school, but you have to okay their choice for church (decided ahead of time). Some of the clothes they pick might not look as "nice" as those you would choose; but as part of their development this issue is not significant enough to warrant a daily negative battle.

Other ways to prevent mishaps and potential negative interactions include the following:

- Put lids on glasses and cups to prevent spills, avoid a mess and, perhaps, prevent an angry outburst from you to your child. Kids feel clumsy and bad about most of their spills and mishaps; we do not need to rub it in.

- With teens, be specific and write down rules and expectations. For example, you might jot down on a memo board by the 'phone, "Dave agrees to be home by 11:00 p.m. with a half tank of gas or no car for two weeks." Then Dave and Dad initial the agreement. This avoids a lot of "I thought you said" remarks and negative name calling such as, "You're so irresponsible. I can't trust you."

If your kids have played together more than 30 minutes and begin getting rowdy, calmly change the direction of their play. You can say, "Okay, it's time for a story. Come and sit with me on the couch." Or, "It's time to paint and play with puzzles and play-dough." A change in play often offsets the typical deterioration in lengthy play periods which can lead to emotional or physical harm to a child.

When you enter a room and activities seem chaotic and out of control, talking in a calm relaxed voice as you redirect the activities often prevents potential negative events. Remove a toy (stick, bat, etc.) that may result in an injury to someone and replace it with a safer toy. Know your child's level of self-control and tolerance for frustration. Do not wait until your preschooler clobbers his friend.

Finally, some children of two-working-parents act out their emotional needs by displaying negative behavior. Perhaps the child's positive behavior is overlooked (not attended to or is ignored). If so, the child may resort to negative behavior such as whining and hitting because they get a predictable, albeit negatively, reinforced response ("Hey, stop that!"). If you work outside the home, when possible take time to give your young children warm, loving nurturance and positive attention in the morning before you go to work. Remember to repeat the same positive attention when you return home.

You might want to note on the following The ABCs of Behavior chart what antecedents (persons, situations, statements, or behaviors) precede your child's behavior. It will be helpful to fill in the chart, but you may choose to just review it.

The ABCs Of Behavior – Sample

STEP 1.   What is one *specific behavior* you would like to change?
Crying when told he has to stop playing to eat or leave for errands.

STEP 2.   What are the usual *antecedents* of (what comes before) this behavior?
He is playing with his toys; engrossed in an activity.

When does it occur? Whenever he's asked to come and eat or leave for errands.

Where does it occur? At home.

With whom does it occur? Usually with Mom.

Other antecedents? Child's temperament, does not like changing activities.

STEP 3.   What are the usual *consequences* of this behavior?
I let him play longer; He is carried to the table crying; his toys are taken away.

STEP 4.   What are the most likely reasons you child is behaving in this way?
He is not given direct commands and there are no consistent consequences.

STEP 5.   What's *another more positive behavior to reward*?
Coming right away when I say we need to eat or leave for errands.

STEP 6.   How might you *change the antecedents* so that the problem behavior is less likely to occur?
Tell Hayden when I begin making lunch that he has 10 more minutes to play. Tell Hayden how much time he has before we leave and remind him he will get a positive point on his chart for immediate obedience. If he chooses not to come, he will loose a point and go to time-out.

STEP 7.   How might you *change the consequences* so that the problem behavior is not rewarded?
Let Hayden know lunch will be ready in five minutes; if he comes immediately, he gets a positive point on his chart; if not, he looses a point and goes to time-out. No negative attention in the form of nagging or yelling is provided.

The ABCs Of Behavior – Form

STEP 1.   What is one *specific behavior* you would like to change?

_____

STEP 2.   What are the usual *antecedents* of (what comes before) this behavior?

_____

When does it occur?

_____

Where does it occur?

_____

With whom does it occur?

_____

Other antecedents?

_____

STEP 3.   What are the usual *consequences* of this behavior?

_____

STEP 4.   What is the most likely reason your child is behaving this way?

STEP 5.   What is *another more positive behavior to reward*?

_____

STEP 6.   How might you *change the antecedents* so that the problem behavior is less likely to occur?

_____

_____

STEP 7.   How might you *change the consequences* so that the problem behavior is not being rewarded?

_____

_____

"C"onsequences Continued: POSITIVE PRAISE, ATTENTION, AND OTHER REINFORCERS

Verbal Praise

Verbal praise is the most versatile type of reinforcement. You have an unlimited repertoire of positive and verbal responses you can make following your child's positive behavior. Examples include: "Thank you for taking your dishes to the sink. I really appreciate the help!" "I see you are taking your time while you color that picture." (Increases and maintains reflective, careful work by the child.) "I like how you show your sister kindness." (Builds and maintains positive sibling relationship.) *Verbal praise should always be given when desirable behaviors occur.* Other rewards and reinforcers may be added at parental discretion.

Material Rewards

These include money, toys, clothes, radio, TV, telephone, car, CDs, CD player, video games, candy, etc. At times parents resort to giving material rewards because this type reward is much easier to give than praise, our time, or *ourselves.* Material rewards are very desirable to our kids, but should be limited. Rewards given should be combined with positive praise.

Activity Rewards

These include taking your child to the park, to a friend's house, reading a book, playing with a favorite toy, riding a bike, going for a walk, going to the store, playing a game with parents, drawing with parents, or art activities. Activity rewards should also be combined with positive praise.

Token Rewards

Anything that can be exchanged for another reinforcer or reward is a token. You can give your child points, happy-face stickers or stars on a chart, chips, pennies, etc. In turn, the child earns material, activity, and other rewards. Token reinforcers should always be given with a social reinforcer such as a hug, pat on the head, smile, etc. Time with parents and significant adults is highly prized by kids. Despite the reasons we give them, kids see things simply: "If I am lovable, you pay attention to me and spend time with me. If you are always gone, preoccupied or only there in body — I must not mean much to you. I'm not worth much." *It is important to make time for positive interaction with your kids every day.*

Social Rewards

Social rewards include, but are not limited to, verbal praise. Any form of positive verbal and/or behavioral approval is considered positive attention. A behavioral approval most children recognize and seek is a look of delightful joy on a parent's face following positive child behavior (coming when asked, trying a new activity). Other forms of positive attention include:

- Watching your child with undivided attention while they do their homework and are on-task (this will increase their on-task behavior).
- Giving them a hug.
- Patting them on the head.
- Giving them a *thumbs up signal*.
- Bestowing a kiss.
- Winking at them.
- Describing what you see the child doing ("I see a boy who is showing self-control." "Now you are putting a green block next to the red one.")

Simply watching your child as they perform positive behaviors will increase those behaviors. Looking away from or ignoring your child when they display minor negative behaviors will decrease those behaviors.

WHAT'S INSIDE YOUR "ANGER CONTAINER?"

Lift the lid of your "boxed-in-thoughts" — your *anger container*. You may discover a jumble of negative feelings: Frustration, guilt, defiance, and extreme stress, among others.

Sorting out this jumble allows you to address issues which jump-start your anger. Note that anger is a response that requires a team-mate; *there is always an underlying issue.* Anyone who has struggled with anger control is aware that the challenge is daunting. However:

Understanding why you react with anger in a given situation with certain people (especially your kids), allows you to learn and practice specific skills to effect change.

Push the Button — Watch the Fireworks!

Visualize a button labeled **Guaranteed Anger Inducer.** Push it and a message reading: **Having to Defend Your Self-Esteem** pops up. Anger is the result of negative feelings teaming-up and verbally racing toward a target: It is an automatic response when we feel our self-esteem is attacked.

Example:

Imagine the lady sitting next to you in a restaurant raises her eyebrow as your 3-year-old crawls under the table. You interpret (mind read) the lady's gesture as implying that you are a "bad" Mother. To protect your self-esteem you react in anger, perhaps jerking your child's arm or yelling, "Stop it!" To control your anger in these situations, do the following:

1. Keep your self-esteem independent of the opinions of others. (This takes practice!)
2. Use coping statements: *"I'll ignore her; I'm doing the best I can." "Stay calm. Do what you need to do." "I'm going to walk him outside and put him in time-out."*
3. Do not mind read: *"Who knows what she's thinking? If she isn't aware of, sympathetic to, or supportive of my efforts, do I care?"*

CHAPTER 5

"ACCENTUATING THE POSITIVE!"

PARENTS, LISTEN UP! POSITIVE PRAISE AND ATTENTION are worth their weight in gold as teaching tools when children are learning appropriate behavior.

As previously noted, parents often say they take my Anger Control Parenting classes to learn the most effective way to *punish* their children's misbehavior. They exclaim they have tried everything (time-out, spanking, restriction, etc.) and nothing works. That is because, as you have learned, *only punishing negative child behaviors is not effective discipline*. Additionally, clinical research and experience have shown that using primarily negative and punitive methods of discipline can:

- Cause the child to withdraw.
- Make a child aggressive.
- Cause the child to suffer poor self-esteem.
- Lead to poor parent-child relationships.

A primary reason your children's negative behavior should be changed with positive, rather than punishing, methods is: Relying solely on punishment for negative behavior only teaches children what *not* to do. For example, shouting at Megan to "Stop that whining, now!" tells her what to stop, *but does not instruct her in how to speak clearly to get what she wants.*

Listen to the average parent and notice they issue more reprimands and negative comments ("Stop that." "Don't do that." "Hey, what did you do that for?"), than positive statements ("Good job, two feet on the floor." "Walk slowly."). Dispensing punishment may be more akin to our nature — or at least seem to take less time — than providing verbal and physical praise and attention. For children to be responsible, self-initiating, and have a healthy self-esteem, a strong feeling of love must flow between parents and children. Love provides the foundation that bonds parents and children: Love is enhanced by praise and attention from parent to child.

If children feel esteemed and loved by their parents, they are more likely to model and assume their parents' values. Hearing a daily outpouring of negative parental comments about how they are missing the mark cannot make a child feel cared for or admired by the parents. Children will likely stop trying to please the parents and resort to turning-off and tuning-out.

Parents often tell children to *behave appropriately*, but may fail to *teach* them appropriate behavior. Though initially skeptical, parents learn they can change their children's behavioral patterns by using positive praise and attention. Consider the following:

> Five-year-old Dylan is pouring a cup of punch and he spills a little. His father sarcastically remarks, "Punch is for drinking, not spilling! If you can't do it right, let someone do it for you." Dylan's negative self-statements probably include, *"I'm dumb! I can't do this by myself. I'll let someone else. He thinks I'm stupid."* Dylan's father could have said, "Good job pouring, here's a paper-towel to wipe up a bit. Sometimes punch spills if the bottle is too heavy." Or, "Would you like me to help you?" This gives the child ideas for choices without affecting his self-esteem.

In the previous negative example, Dylan was not encouraged to try a new skill. Instead, he was shamed for making a mistake. Over time, negative comments such as these will teach Dylan not to try at all. He will be reluctant to take a chance, fearing he will be shamed for his errors.

Parents at times are unaware of the damaging effect their negative comments have on their children. Listen carefully to your words and tone of voice: Concentrate on positives! Focusing on praising and paying attention to desired behaviors is important for reasons other than reducing or eliminating unwanted behaviors:

- Children receiving affirmations about how valuable they are to the family and how much they are loved and appreciated are more likely to want to please their parents.

- These kids want to keep the positive parental comments and gestures coming their way. They learn to value their parents as a significant source of love and attention.

For healthy emotional growth and family harmony, parents must cultivate the habit of praising and attending to their children's positive behavior.

Following is a format designed to monitor how often you punish, praise, or direct your child's behavior. You might want to jot down comments to review at a later time:

Self Monitoring Chart - Comments I Make To My Child				
	Neutral	Positive	Negative	Directive (Do)
Monday				
Tuesday				
Wednesday				
Thursday				
Friday				
Saturday				
Sunday				

SPECIFIC PRAISE VERSUS NON-SPECIFIC PRAISE

"Spell It Out" — Specific Praise

Specific positive verbal praise tells the child exactly what you like about their behavior: "It makes me happy when I see you share your toys with your sister." Or, "I really like to see you share your toys with your sister." Or "Building blocks can be frustrating. I like your self-control." Children learn best when the behavior to be increased is specifically praised. Being *specific* about the behavior tells the child exactly what behavior you like and they are more likely to repeat it.

"Generic Praise Is Nice, But . . ." — Non-Specific Praise

Saying, "Great job!" makes it more difficult for the child to learn specifically what they're being praised for. For example, if Mom walked into the kitchen just as *Jason and Marisa* finished doing the dishes and said "Nice job!" the kids would not be sure if she was praising the way they did the dishes, how they cooperated, or that they finished on time. It is possible that brother and sister hit each other or argued during the work process, in which case they won't feel as if they deserve the praise.

You might praise as follows: "When you do the dishes it makes me feel good that you help." Or, "I appreciate it when you do the dishes when you are supposed to." When kids share a drawing or project they made, parents have a tendency to remark with a general statement like, "That's nice" or "Aha." Again, it may not be clear to the child what specifically you like about the picture or project. Try and find something you like which you can describe, such as the colors or the design. Or simply describe what you see (much like you do in the child's focus time). Example: "I see you used black and green colors here and you put a blue triangle over there. That's neat."

In general, phrases like *good girl* or *good boy* evaluate the entire person rather than just their behavior. Mom may walk into the family room and say, "What good kids!" though two minutes before they were calling each other names. They may feel the compliment was undeserved and may even feel a bit deceptive. Instead, upon seeing the kids sitting nicely together, Mom could say, "I see you are sitting together nicely watching TV. That's great." She is paying positive attention to a desired behavior (sitting without fighting) by describing that behavior.

Examples of Specific Praise:

1. "It really makes me happy when you come as soon as I tell you!"
2. "I appreciate it when you listen to what I say."
3. "I like the way you took your time writing your letters."
4. "Opening a new jar can be challenging — boy, you keep on trying!"
5. "I like the way you colored the tree with green and yellow leaves."
6. "Nice job cleaning up your toys!"
7. "Wow, you're trying to think of a lot of solutions to that problem."
8. "I like how you made that snowflake; can you show me how?"

9. "Your desk looks great! You really thought about where to put each thing."

10. "Hey, you marked down the books you read without my help! That's what I call responsibility!"

11. "You're making guesses; that's how we stretch our brain!" (This encourages risk-taking.)

12. "Thank you for putting your game away; that makes my job easier."

13. "I really like that song you just played/sang; can you do it again?"

14. "It makes me so happy when you share with your brother."

15. "Sharing a new toy can be hard; that's what I call generous!"

16. "Tying sister's shoe helps Mommy, and shows Susie you care about her. Thanks!"

17. "You wrote your homework assignment down. That's showing responsibility!"

18. "Waiting so long can really get boring; I appreciate your patience!"

19. "It can be frustrating when blocks fall off your tower. Wow, you're showing self-control and persistence!"

20. "Saying 'no' when other kids are doing something wrong isn't easy. I'm very proud of you."

21. "You called Sara on the phone by yourself. That's really brave."

22. "I'm having fun playing this game with you."

23. "That is what I call obedience, coming to dinner as soon as I called you."

24. "I like your manners while you're eating; it makes me feel as if you care about me."

Examples of Non-Specific Praise:

As mentioned, children learn quickest when we specifically identify and praise a desired behavior. However, non-specific praise can also be used to promote a positive relationship, communicate positive regard, and increase the child's self-esteem. Often the positive behavior being praised will be obvious.

When parents use a variety of ways to praise, their children's attention is captured; otherwise, they may only half-listen. My son said to me one day, "Mom, when I show you something, you always say, "Uh huh!" I immediately understood what he was telling me: He did not think I was interested in or fascinated by his new discoveries since my remark was always the same. The following list shows several ways to express interest in your child. Let the list serve as a guide: Think of other "ways to praise" and use them! Both you and your child will benefit.

1.   Holding your arms out to pick up the child.
2.   Asking them to come over and sit on your lap or sit next to you.
3.   Going up to your child several times a day and hugging and/ or kissing them.
4.   Ruffling their hair or patting their head.
5.   Holding their hands while walking with them.
6.   Telling your child you are happy they are in your family, and happy that they are your child. Telling them they bring you happiness.

Remember: Physical closeness and affection are needed and desired by all children, no matter what outward signals they project.

PRAISE: "A Little Is Good — A Lot Is Better!"

"Name That Behavior" — Reinforce Specifically

Children learn more quickly when you pinpoint and express the behaviors you like or dislike. It is important for a parent to recognize the difference between specific and nonspecific verbal praise (McMahon & Forehand, 1981). An example of general or nonspecific praise is saying, "Nice!" as you walk into the family room and your children are coloring together quietly. Though the children may like the comment, they will not know whether you are praising them for their art work, their cooperation, or something else. Children will repeat the desired behavior more readily with *specific* verbal praise. For example, "It makes me happy to see you sharing the coloring book so nicely." Or, "I really like that cooperation."

"Do It Now" — Reinforce Immediately

Children learn new behaviors faster when the reinforcement immediately follows the desired behavior. Verbally express to your children what behavior you like as soon as they do it. If you wait to tell them what they did correctly, the praise will have little effect on increasing the desired behavior. Example: "Thanks, Ashley for coming home five minutes before your curfew."

"Keep It Up" — Reinforce Continuously

To increase positive behavior, reinforce it each time the behavior occurs. After the behavior occurs at the rate you desire — say, six out of seven days the dishes are brought to the sink — you can switch to intermittent reinforcement. With intermittent reinforcement, you reward the behavior every now and then. Once the behavior is well established, children will continue to show the behavior though they are only randomly reinforced.

VARIETY PUSHES BOREDOM ASIDE — Change Reinforcements

Children can become bored quickly. Recognize when your program is not working because the reinforcement provided is not motivating your child. For example, happy-faces on a chart might motivate the child for a week or so, but after that they fail to influence the child's positive behavior. It is important to vary types of reinforcers: Keep a stock of different types of reinforcers ready to dispense.

LEARN TO MEASURE: "Not Too Much — Not Too Little"

Obtaining the behavioral results you want requires that you provide the correct amount of reinforcement. Too much or too little reinforcement may limit how much the behavior changes. Giving a child too many points or too many favors following the behavior may cause problems. The child may always expect a large payoff for each behavior, making it difficult to phase out the reinforcement.

The goal is to give the child a reasonable reward at first, immediately following each behavior. Gradually, more and more behaviors are required before the reward is given. If too much is given too soon, it will be difficult to get the child to eventually work harder for less.

Do not wait too long to give reinforcements, and do not require a child to perform a behavior too many times before giving reinforcement: The child may give up or not try at all. Be prepared to make adjustments in your reinforcement schedule. You will know if the event is still reinforcing to the child if the frequency of the desired behavior increases. Examine the following if the desired behavior does not occur more often:

1. Does the reinforcer still motivate the child? (Is it too small? Is it too large? Is it too familiar?)

2. Are you reinforcing immediately after the behavior occurs?

3. Are you reinforcing consistently (every time the behavior occurs)?

4. Did you reinforce the behavior each time it occurred (continuously), and then every other time (intermittently)?

Behavior Chart

Child's Name _____

Person(s) Recording Behavior _____

Dates _____ through _____

	Monday	Tuesday	Wednesday	Thursday	Friday	Saturday	Sunday
Positive Behaviors↓							
1.							
2.							
3.							
Total Positive Points→							
Negative Behaviors↓							
1.							
2.							
3.							
Total Negative Points→							
Grand Total *Positive Minus Negative Points*→							

Consequences:
(Points)

+15
+10
+ 5
  0
- 5
- 10
- 15

Time Out For:

1. _____

2. _____

3. _____

TAKING ANOTHER "LOOK" AT REINFORCERS

Recall that a reinforcer is an event that follows a behavior and increases the chance the behavior will recur. For example: Mitzi cries when Mother says, "No" to her request for a cookie. Mitzi then starts an anger tantrum, after which Mom gives her the cookie. Mitzi's tantrum behavior was followed by something positive (a cookie). Thus, the next time Mom says, "No," there is a greater chance Mitzi will tantrum.

Generally, events that are experienced as positive or desirable to the child (attention, praise) will tend to increase behaviors they follow. In contrast, if you remove praise and attention (ignore the child), the rate of positive or negative behavior will occur less frequently. To determine whether you are reinforcing or punishing a behavior, determine whether the behavior increases or decreases. *You influence your child's desirable behaviors by immediate reinforcement.*

REINFORCERS: All Forms, Sizes, Shapes, and Colors!

Positive reinforcers can be anything your child likes, needs, or wants. There are basically four categories of reinforcers. Read the remainder of this section, and then make a list of possible reinforcers for your child. Next, rate the degree to which your child would be motivated to earn such a reinforcer.

Social Reinforcers: These are the more important reinforcers and should be paired with all others. They include smiles, praise, positive attention, and being physically close.

Token Reinforcers: These include anything that can be exchanged for another reinforcer (chips, money, points, tickets, happy-faces stickers); they are always given with a social reinforcer such as a hug, pat on the head, smile, etc.

Activity Reinforcers: Events children find pleasurable include: going to the park, reading a book, playing a game with Mom or Dad, drawing, or coloring.

Material Reinforcers: Tangible rewards such as toys, clothes, money, and snacks make good material reinforcers.

Also, a powerful and desired reinforcer is: **Parents' Time and Attention.** Tickets can be cashed in for a specific amount of Mother's and Father's time. For example, the ticket earned is used to play basketball with Dad for one-half hour.

Social reinforcers should always be given along with token, activity, and material rewards.

Get creative: Think of and list positive reinforcers you can give your child.

MATERIAL:
New toy, compact disk, clothes
_____
_____

SOCIAL:
Smile, hug, praise, positive attention
_____
_____

TOKEN:
Pennies
Tickets
Tally marks
_____

ACTIVITY:
Go to park
Book read by Mom
Watch TV
Bed one hour later
Friend over
_____
_____
_____

OTHER:
_____
_____
_____
_____

AVOID "CABOOSING" AND "OVERDOING" PRAISE

Parents often tag on a negative comment following praise. For example, "Matt, I really like how you put your shoes in order in your closet. Why can't you keep it that way every day?" That ending comment, in effect, cancels out the praise. Parents may say they are simply taking the opportunity to teach the child. However, children are often left feeling put down and upset following a caboose statement. This reduces their motivation to learn anything.

Too much praise can also backfire. In an effort to build their children up, some well-meaning parents praise too much. Every time Ryan Michelle does or makes something, Dad showers her with lavish praise. "Oh, that is an incredible drawing! You're the best artist I know!" Every day as Mom readies Ryan Michelle for pre-school, Mom says, "You look so beautiful!"

A child's self-esteem can actually be reduced by *too much praise* for average daily performance. The child becomes dependent on large doses of praise and when it is not forthcoming from peers or other adults, they feel rejected or inadequate. They may also develop a false sense of competency in areas where they are average or below average. Children may maintain a false self-image, fearing the possibility of losing parental attention or approval. This could set them up for later problems and disappointments. **Praise should be offered specifically and *realistically* regarding behaviors or attitudes you like or admire.**

Girls often feel they must *look good* to be valued; boys usually gain accolades for *looking buff*. You might try praising your child for such attributes as *kindness*, *generosity*, and *helpfulness*, rather than emphasizing physical appearance. Of course, moderation is key. It is okay to say how nice your child looks from time to time: It is a matter of degree and emphasis.

THE VALUE OF PRAISING — Cost: Nothing. Worth: A Lot!

Focusing on praising and attending to desired behaviors is important for reasons other than reducing or eliminating unwanted behaviors. Research has shown that using positive methods to teach children appropriate behavior enhances their self-esteem and also fosters a positive parent-child relationship.

Kids receiving daily affirmations about how valuable they are and experiencing how much they are appreciated and loved are more likely to want to please their parents. They want to keep the positives coming: Parents are valued as a significant source of positives.

Studies show that kids who hear mostly negative comments lose their incentive to obey. They perceive their parents are usually disappointed in their behavior and do not value them. There is little feeling of being cherished or valued and these children feel hopeless about learning different behaviors.

Children often see themselves as their parents see them and develop their self-concept, in part, from their parents. Your children may think that you do not like or love them because you exhibit disapproval for most of what they say and do. The danger is that they may internalize this as disgust or self-hate.

The goal is to teach your children desired behaviors. But, you also must allow them to feel they are always valued and loved though some of their behaviors are unacceptable. Children must believe and experience that you think they can perform the desired behaviors. In disciplining their children, parents must learn to use methods that teach their child positive behaviors, while simultaneously safeguarding the child's self-esteem.

A positive approach to parenting allows the parent-child relationship to stay warm and close; this is a necessary prerequisite for internalizing parental values. Children are more likely to model and take on their parent's values and opinions if there is a close parent-child bond. Children who encounter mostly negative comments and a lot of "No's," sarcasm, and negative attention have little reason for pleasing the parent. What is more, if the flow of negative comments remains constant such kids may try to avoid the negative parent altogether. Kids who are subjected to this environment are likely to model their parent's negativity, but not buy into their parent's positive values.

"IGNORING" IS NOT A NATURAL PARENTAL TRAIT

A behavior is weakened when the reinforcing "C"onsequence is removed. This is a form of extinction or what is commonly called *ignoring*. When a behavior is followed by the absence of a reward or attention, the frequency of the behavior will decrease over time. For example:

Five-year-old Tommy looks at his Mom and lets his spit drool. Mom calmly turns away and busies herself doing something else, as if unaware of Tommy's action. Tommy's inappropriate behavior was not reinforced by negative attention in the form of, "Oh, Tommy, that's disgusting!" *Ignoring can be used for minor misbehavior.*

Forehand & McMahon (1981) and other researchers suggest that to ignore effectively and thereby decrease a negative behavior, you must:

1. **Stay calm and remain positive.**
2. **Have no eye contact with the child.**
3. **Turn your face away so that you do not inadvertently roll your eyes or shake your head in disgust or disapproval.**
4. **Do not speak to your child. Any form of attention is still attention and will increase or maintain the negative behavior. Do not say, "I'm ignoring you." Any verbal response is still a form of attention and will increase the behavior it follows.**
5. **Remove physical attention. You are not completely**

ignoring whining or tantrums when you pick up and hold your child.

6. Consistently ignore the inappropriate behavior. That is, ignore it every time it occurs. If you pay attention to the negative behavior every now and then, you essentially "lock it in."

If Emily whines and gets what she wants from time to time, she will whine every time you say, "No." She has learned that sometimes she gets what she wants by whining.

Behaviors to ignore include tantrums, crying in bed until the parent comes in, and complaining.

Behaviors not **to ignore** include any form of negative physical contact such as hitting, pushing, kicking, or damaging physical property.

(Remember to *praise the opposite positive behavior!*)

Ignoring May Reach Dizzying Heights — Stay Balanced!

When you ignore a previously reinforced behavior (child crying in the crib when put to bed), the behavior often gets much worse before it gets better. Eighteen-month-old Aubrey usually cried after her parents put her to bed at night. Feeling sorry for her, they would go in and pick her up. Every time they put her back down she would cry. After two or three times, they lost their patience and yelled at her. Other times they would let her sleep with them. Using ignoring to change this pattern required determined resolve and commitment by the parents to not give in.

The first night of the program Aubrey cried loudly 20 minutes. The parents were instructed to put Aubrey to bed and let her cry. After 15 minutes they stuck their head in her room and said that it was bedtime, she had to go to sleep and they were not going to pick her up. She cried even harder and louder the next 15 minutes, banging her head against the crib, and throwing all the bedding on the floor.

Again, her parents repeated the procedure. They did not comment on the banging of her head against the crib or bedding thrown out of the crib. This process continued up to three hours the first night until Aubrey got physically exhausted and fell asleep. As you become more predictable and consistent in disciplining your children, they will learn that you *mean what you say* and that protesting and battling does not pay off.

"IGNORING" — A Tool to Be Used Sparingly

Knowing when and how to ignore takes skill. For this reason, I *recommend using it only when you expect it to work.* For example, if you ignore swearing or words used by 3- to 6-year-olds such as "You're a poop!" and the inappropriate verbiage does not decrease or increases, then ignoring, for whatever reason, is not working. You may want to use some other form of mild punishment (time-out, privilege loss, or a tiny (*very tiny*!) amount of soap in the mouth combined with time-out).

Learn when you need to ignore sibling conflict and when to intervene. Generally, let one or two interchanges pass to see if they can *work it out*. Otherwise, remind them "If you can't work it out, you'll have to sit on the chair. Do you want my help in solving your problem or can you figure it out for yourselves?"

Effective ignoring requires you to ignore the behavior every time it occurs; do not rely on this method unless you can be consistent. Otherwise, try other suggested measures. As soon as positive behavior occurs (showing self-control after tantrum) praise and attend to your child.

The point of ignoring is: To remove all attention and rewards when negative behavior occurs, and to praise and attend when appropriate behavior occurs. (Look away when your child is purposely drooling spit; hug them or give positive verbal attention as soon as the drooling stops.)

ANGER PROVOKING THINKING PATTERNS:

"WHAT WAS I THINKING?"

As mentioned previously, *it is not the external event that makes you angry but the way you **think** about the event.* What does the event mean to you? How do you view it? What you think about the anger situation is often distorted or twisted in some way. That is, the way you are viewing the event may not be objectively correct and, therefore, leads to increased anger.

Listed below are some common errors in thinking that could increase your anger. Once you recognize and evaluate the anger inducing errors in your thinking, you can correct them. Then, you will see how your anger melts away. Dr. Aaron Beck and others have identified that depressed persons engage in the following distortions. Individuals with anger problems also demonstrate these errors in thinking.

Labeling

When you label a person, you negatively categorize the total person. Rather than "My son needs to learn better self-control," you label him and say, "He's a monster!" Rather than "She isn't compliant when I ask her to do something," you exclaim, "She's such a brat!" When we label our children we overlook all their positive qualities and see only the negative. Being a *monster* or a *brat* is difficult to change, but kids can be taught how to be more compliant and how to increase self-control. Parents may show anger more readily by negatively labeling the whole person. Thinking that their child is a *brat* or a *monster* may cause parents to feel injured or cheated.

To reduce your angry feelings toward your child, focus on what they *did* and not what you feel they *are*. Remind yourself that your child has many attributes: good, bad, and neutral. What goes around comes around: When you view your child in only negative terms, they also may feel angry and that angry attitude may reinforce the negative view you have of them. A child's negative behaviors can be changed if you are committed to following a consistent program. But, *locking our children in rigid roles seriously limits their potential to achieve.*

Mind Reading

Parents often assume what their child is thinking and conclude *why* they did a particular deed. For example: "He's running away from me just to embarrass me!" Two-year-old Tommy may just want to continue playing and needs a consequence for noncompliance. You may conclude, "She just wants that toy because her sister has it." She may just want the toy.

Children are always testing their relative social power. Kids must be taught to cope with social power differences and how to share. Take time to focus on the behavior: Don't guess your child's intention; you may be wrong.

"How many times have I told you not to climb on the counter tops? You always deliberately disobey me! Now get down!" Feeling misunderstood and dejected, 4-year-old Jason climbs down. If staying off the counter tops was a current behavior Mother was trying to reduce, she could have said, "The rule is stay off the counter tops. You lose one point and go to time-out." If Jason protests, "But I was trying to get the scissors for you," Mother can thank him; but at least a point should be taken away so he learns, "I can't ever climb up on the counter tops."

We've all scolded our children after jumping to the conclusion that they did something for a selfish reason, only to find they were trying to help. Knowing Mom was looking for the scissors, 4-year-old Jason climbed up on the counter top to get them for her. Mom walked into the kitchen, saw Jason, and assumed he was purposely disobeying the rule not to climb on the counter tops.

Black and White Thinking

With black and white thinking, you view your children and their behavior in absolute and extreme terms. "She **never**," "He **always**," is often uttered when you describe your children's behavior. Similar to labeling, you over-generalize reality, seeing and describing your child's behavior in a negatively distorted way. Black and white thinking increases the likelihood you will become angry, just as labeling does. Compare: "He never listens," to "I need to set up a chart to increase your obeying." Or, "I have let you get away with not listening to me when I speak to you," could be changed to "I need to teach you to listen."

When you blame your child for their noncompliance, your sense of fairness and justice tells you that it is their fault they are causing you misery. Feeling victimized, you become angry and lash out. A parent's responsibility includes teaching their children the behavior they want them to display. Parents must hold children accountable for desired behaviors by enforcing prearranged consequences.

Magnification/Minimization

With this type distortion, you exaggerate the negative and downplay the positive. We often ignore or forget our children's positive behaviors, focusing more on the negative. This viewpoint can make your child's problems seem more difficult, frequent, and hopeless to change. Parents also tend to remember a child's negative, ineffective discipline actions and take for granted or overlook positive outcomes. You may start off by staying calm and giving a clear, direct command for your child to come to you. However, your son ignores you and you get angry and grab his arm. Remembering later that you overreacted emotionally brings on a guilt feeling; this realization leaves you with a hopeless feeling about your ability to control your anger and discipline effectively. If this happens, you may consider abandoning your ACP program.

More balanced/objective thinking allows you to acknowledge what you did right and identifies what went wrong in this situation. You can determine what you need to do differently the next time. In the first example, the distorted thinking can lead to feelings of depression. More balanced thinking will allow you to feel encouraged and hopeful about your ability to learn from your mistakes and to make necessary changes.

Over-Generalization

When you over-generalize, you erroneously reason that because one particular event happened, this pattern or behavior always happens. You view yourself, the world, and your child's behavior through a negative distorted lens. You often see, expect, and remember only the negative. You think, "He can't control himself," then expect confirming evidence instead of looking for, teaching, and reinforcing the opposite positive behaviors when they occur.

Fortune Telling

Resorting to fortune telling, you might whisper in 3-year-old Dylan's ear to not put his finger in the birthday cake. As the cake is placed near him, he struggles to keep his hands down. Mother says, "That's great self-control. I like how you're keeping your hands by your side." Dylan is encouraged to continue keeping his hands down. Incidentally, Mother should learn Dylan's limit for self-control. She might allow him to briefly practice "hands down by side" and then hold him on her lap or move him to another location (away from the cake).

You assume that things will turn out badly without any concrete reason or evidence. For instance, you anticipate: "She won't sit still in church." "He will act up at the restaurant." You start out feeling hopeless and defeated instead of planning how you will handle a potential negative behavior or situation.

Emotional Reasoning

With emotional reasoning, you reason based on what you *feel* is true. You *feel* as if you are a *lousy* parent and conclude that you are one. You *feel* as if you *can't* handle the current situation so you do not attempt to stay calm and implement your plan. You *feel* too tired so you conclude that you can't put the kids in time-out. If you "Just do it!" you will demonstrate to yourself that you can do many things despite how you feel. When you hear yourself say, *I feel I am such a failure* (and you believe that you are): Look for evidence to support the opposite. Mind-list your accomplishments or why you are a good parent — or write them down. Over time, you will notice that your negative feelings about yourself, your child, or the situation seldom reflect reality.

Just as adults can evoke angry responses from us, so can our children. But we must realize that children's intentions and reasons for doing what they do differ from those of adults. Normally, children do things daily that frustrate and irritate us. Example: It is not uncommon for children to dawdle when getting out of a car, if something draws their attention. Mastering the skill of relaxation and anger control helps us to cope with such anger evoking behaviors. By reacting calmly, we will keep our stress level low and safeguard our children's self-esteem.

HOW YOUR THINKING MAKES YOU ANGRY

To review: The way you think about or view a situation determines whether you become angry as well as determining your anger level. You have learned to clarify what thoughts go through your mind during challenging discipline situations. You have learned that many of these thoughts do not reflect an objective view of *reality*: They are distorted or biased, usually reflecting *your issues*.

Recall the categories of distorted thinking and store the following in your memory bank:

- Your irrational thinking patterns can make you angry.
- Thinking calmly can help you to control your anger.

ANGER PROVOKING THINKING PATTERNS

1. **All-or-none thinking:** You look at things in absolute, black and white categories.
2. **Over-generalization:** You view a negative event as a never-ending pattern of defeat.
3. **Mental filter:** You dwell on the negatives and ignore the positives.
4. **Discounting the positives:** You insist that your accomplishments or positive qualities *do not count.*
5. **Jumping to conclusions:** (a) Mind reading — you assume people are reacting negatively to you when there is no definite evidence for this. (b) Fortune-telling — you arbitrarily predict that things will turn out badly.
6. **Magnification or minimization:** You blow things out of proportion or you shrink their importance inappropriately.
7. **Emotional reasoning:** You reason from how you feel: "I feel like an idiot, so I really must be one." Or, "I don't feel like doing this, so I'll put it off."
8. **"Should" statements:** You self-criticize or criticize others with *should's* or *shouldn'ts; must's, ought's,* and *have to's.*
9. **Labeling:** You identify with your shortcomings. Instead of saying, "I made a mistake," you tell yourself, "I'm a jerk," or "a fool," or "a loser."
10. **Personalizing the blame:** You blame yourself for something you weren't entirely responsible for, or you blame other people and overlook ways that your attitudes and behaviors might contribute to a problem.
11. **Blaming your child:** A natural tendency is to blame our anger on someone or something else, rather than taking responsibility for it. Surveying your anger diaries might reveal your tendency to focus on what your child did to you, and how you feel they intentionally and knowingly did/didn't do something that made you angry.

A first step to lasting change in your anger patterns is: Taking responsibility for how your children behave.

For example, perhaps you have repeatedly told Kianne to take her clothes and books to her room and not to leave them "where she drops them." Yet, she usually drops them and leaves them where they fall. "She's nine and she should know better," you protest. "Sometimes, I think she does it just to annoy me; that's why I yell. She drives me to it!"

If Kianne is still dropping her clothes and books and not putting them in a proper place, that indicates she has not been *taught* to do otherwise. There has not been a large enough consequence assessed and enforced to make her choose to *remember* to put her clothes and books where they belong. The bottom line: She has not developed the habit you want her to develop.

If you continue to blame her and assume she is *refusing to remember* just to annoy you, each infraction sets you up to lash out in anger. Alternatively, if you accept that you haven't *taught* her the desired habit, you can turn your energy and focus toward constructing a new plan. Being task oriented is one way to reduce your anger.

CHANGING YOUR THINKING PATTERNS

BRIEF ACCOUNT OF THE EVENT	THOUGHTS DURING THE EVENT	WHAT THE BEHAVIOR MEANS TO ME	MY EXPECTATIONS	MORE RATIONAL THOUGHTS
Talked back when asked to do chores.	*"Why can't she do it without talking back? Why can't she just do it?"*	She doesn't respect me.	Do it without talking back.	*"Kids are independent and do not want to be told what to do. Don't take it personal. Just put her into time-out for talking back and mark off a point."*
Kids fighting.	*"Why can't I read my magazine without them always fighting?"*	They are being inconsiderate and don't care about me. I don't matter.	When reading, I should not be interrupted by kids fighting.	*"They are fighting. What intervention can I use to reduce/ stop the fighting?"*
Running away in a store in front of other parents.	*"He is such a brat, he never listens."*	He is doing this to embarrass me.	He should always stay by my side.	*"Two year olds will run. I need to prevent his running by keeping him buckled into the cart and/or set up predictable consequences ahead of time; like earning his privileges for staying by me."*
Why are the kids always bickering when we are in the car?	*"They do this to upset me. They don't care about my feelings."*	Why do they always bicker in the car? It disturbs my driving.	The kids should not bicker in the car.	*"Kids are going to bicker. How do I train them to resolve their conflicts with less bickering?"*

CHANGING YOUR THINKING PATTERNS FORM

BRIEF ACCOUNT OF THE EVENT	THOUGHTS DURING THE EVENT	WHAT THE BEHAVIOR MEANS TO ME	MY EXPECTATIONS	MORE RATIONAL THOUGHTS

CHAPTER 6

"SHOWTIME: TURN ON THAT SPOTLIGHT!"

Previous chapters focused on various teaching and learning experiences set in motion and directed by parents. This chapter highlights fun-time/playtime activities staged and acted out between parents and child. **The twist:** *The child is the star in the spotlight and also the director who chooses the script.* **Parents are — for a short time — relegated to a supporting role.** An initial challenge for parents may be to accept this new role with enthusiasm and refrain from "taking over" the activity. FIRST, parents must realize that:

"IT'S NOT ALWAYS ABOUT *YOU!*"

So, *Who* is *"It"* About and *What* is *"It"*? — Child-Centered Play

The **child** is the center of attention. **Child-Centered play** (CCP) was originally conceptualized by Drs. Hanf & Kling (1973) and Drs. Forehand & McMahon (1981). We have adapted CCP here as an activity period designed to:

- Improve your relationship with your child.
- Provide an opportunity for you to practice giving positive praise and attention to your child.
- Build your child's self-esteem.

During this scheduled playtime, **parents resist taking the lead and focus on the child**. They practice and follow a script initiated by the child. This activity period provides a stage for building and strengthening a positive parent-child relationship and for increasing their child's self-esteem. It will be easier for parents to adjust as they notice the rewards for their commitment, time, and patience.

When playing with their child, parents typically structure the activity. They suggest the playtime setting and generate rules, turning the occasion into an opportunity to teach their child. Questions are asked throughout the activity, causing the child to follow rather than lead. Such questions interrupt the child's flow of activity and creativity. Structuring your child's play activity, asking questions, and teaching are all appropriate. **However, a much different interaction is created when the child is the featured player/director.**

Allow your child to select an activity, perhaps with building blocks/Legos, coloring books or paints. For older kids, you might watch and encourage as they practice a sport or play a video game. Keep your focus and attention on what they are doing and practice praising their efforts. Communicate verbally and non-verbally that you enjoy being with them and are delighted by what they are doing.

At first, your child might be surprised that you are so interested in what they are doing. They may not be used to your spending such focused time with them. Some children ask, "Why are you talking and acting so funny?" Just tell them that you like watching them play. Your child will display more initiative as they make choices and direct the activities. Too, parents often report feeling joyful in discovering child behaviors they can comment on positively.

For some children, a designated playtime focused on them may be the only time during the day when their parents seem to "like" them and react positively to their behavior. Some parents say they feel awkward and uncomfortable under this arrangement. Perhaps they feel so negative toward their child they find it difficult to praise them. However, you can always find something positive to say about what your child is doing ("You are taking your time putting that block on top of the other one. I like that.").

Many parents reported the results of this spotlight time with their children were so rewarding, they continued to schedule time to watch their "stars shine." Parents noted their child's positive behaviors increased and their negative behaviors decreased. Both children and parents looked forward to their special role-reversal time together. This is a good example of: Giving more positives and receiving more positives in return.

Goals and rules for CCP are summarized below and provide a handy reference for future use. Try to make a personal commitment to play 5-20 minutes per day, especially the first 2-4 weeks of your new program. Record — or keep a mental note of — the number of minutes you and your child were *on stage*. Then, you can gauge if the modified playtime influenced your child's behavior that day. Audio or videotaping these play periods is an excellent way to view your child's reactions. This also allows you to make any necessary changes in your behavior. For example, were you asking questions or not showing enough enthusiasm?

By trading your *director's chair* for a *producer's role*, you will *produce*:

A "WIN/WIN" SITUATION

- Parent learns to observe and notice positive child behaviors.
- Parent learns to give praise and attention following appropriate child behavior.
- Parent learns to ignore minor inappropriate child behavior.
- Child learns what to do instead of a negative behavior ("Use your words, don't hit.").
- Parent becomes a more positive reinforcer to the child.
- Child will want to obey to please parent.
- Parent-child relationship becomes more positive, warm, and intimate.
- Child's self-esteem will increase.

RULES FOR CHILD-CENTERED PLAY:

RULE	PURPOSE	EXAMPLE
1. Child selects activity.	Child learns to feel comfortable making decisions. Child experiences that she or he is valued enough to be listened to and watched, increasing self-esteem.	Activities could include: Playing with Legos, building blocks, playing Nintendo, manipulating a transformer, or painting pictures.
2. Parent focuses on child and follows child's lead. Parent does not change activity.	Child learns to lead an activity. Child learns to take initiative; decisions are respected.	Child: "We are driving to the fire. Put your man in front, Mom." Parent does as child says and continues to follow child's play. Parent's eyes are focused on child and what they are doing. Parent smiles and shows they are interested and engaged in the activity

RULE	PURPOSE	EXAMPLE
3. Parent describes step by-step what child does.	Communicates that you're interested in what they're doing. You're with them every step. Teaches child to identify and label their emotions and feelings. Allows parent to practice being at child's level. (This is the first step toward building open communication when they are teenagers!)	"I see that you're moving the space man down and over." "You seem frustrated, but you're controlling your hands." (Child is encouraged to choose self-control vs. throwing blocks.) "You're putting red blocks on top of the green block."
4. Parent participates in child's play on child's level.	Shows genuine interest in what child is doing. Child sees that parent likes to do what the child does vs. parent telling child how to play. Shows that parent enjoys being with them. Child is listened to and feels their play choices are good ideas, since parent is following.	Keeping attention focused on child, parent builds town next to child. Participates in doll play, but follows child's lead and praises child. Parent still reflects, describes, and shows they like to spend time with their child.
5. Parent uses reflective feedback and answers child's questions.	Communicates that parent heard what child said. Can clarify child's feelings, wishes, etc.	Child: "I can't get the hat to stay on." Parent: "It's not easy to keep that hat on."
6. Parent gives praise for appropriate behavior.	Fosters close parent/child relationship. Parent communicates with love. Teaches child what behaviors are desirable. Increases likelihood that child's positive behaviors will be repeated.	Parent: "You're taking your time drawing the hair. You're really concentrating before you make your move. I like those colors."

RULE	PURPOSE	EXAMPLE
7. Parent does not criticize.	Keeps interaction positive. Eliminates negative attention that might increase negative behaviors. Child feels free to take risks and make mistakes. Secures child's self-esteem.	Child: "I can't color in the lines." Parent: "Coloring can be frustrating at times. I'm proud of you for taking time to stick with it."
8. Parent ignores inappropriate behavior. (Unless it is dangerous or destructive.) Parent removes reinforcement for less serious negative behavior (and thereby decreases the behavior).	Child learns that praise and attention only follow positive behavior.	Child tosses a toy and looks at Dad for reaction. Dad ignores action, acts as if he didn't see it. As soon as child resumes playing appropriately, Dad praises efforts in building and says, "This is sure fun."
9. Do not ask child questions ("Why do the truck's wheels turn like that?").	Takes child's focus from their preferred activity and interrupts thought process. Interrupts flow of child's activity. Parent is trying to lead vs. follow.	Parent: "I see you are placing the blocks in the truck." (Do not ask why.) Child may comment or just smile because you are watching.
10. Do not give commands ("Build a big bridge."), unless behavior is dangerous or destructive. Use observation comments.	Parent is leading. The goal is to follow the child.	Parent: "Oh, I see you want to put the cars together." "You are using color pens instead of crayons. That is a different way to color."
11. Do not teach, as the parent, not child, then structures activity. May elicit a negative response if child can't answer correctly.	Purpose of this exercise is to allow child to lead, not to learn new knowledge. Child must stop their desired activity to follow yours. Puts pressure on the child to perform and search for a correct answer.	Parent: "You are dressing your doll all by yourself." "I like how you do that with patience, stacking the blocks slowly and doing a nice job."

At the end of the day, many parents/caregivers may say to themselves:

"Tomorrow, I will try harder to not yell at or criticize my child."
"Tomorrow, I will set aside extra time to interact with my child."
"Tomorrow, I will listen more closely to my child."
"Tomorrow, I will practice anger control and be more understanding."

The only thing better than making those changes *tomorrow* is making them *today*!

ANGER IS A PROCESS:

Controlling our anger may be easier if we *understand* the process. Dr. Raymond Novaco (1976) theorizes that anger incidents appear to go through four stages. Knowing which stage you are in can increase your sense of control over the situation.

Stage 1 — Preparing For Provocation

A potentially anger-evoking situation has just occurred. You are able to define the problem and begin generating potential solutions. You can determine all possible antecedents that could be prevented in future. At this stage it is easier to control your anger. As you approach the situation, you are in the best position to think clearly and stay calm.

Stage 2 — Impact and Confrontation

You have passed through Stage 1, and the problem wasn't resolved quickly as in the example in Stage 1. Instead, James insists that he had the truck first and he wants it back now. He doesn't want to wait for Diane to take a turn first. Mom's anger increases; she feels frustrated that James won't back down and go along with the time-out solution suggested. Notice her self-talk and how her anger escalates. She recognizes her irrational thinking pattern and uses her coping statement to stay mentally focused and physically calm. Rather than staying engaged in the conflict, Mom keeps the chain of interaction short: Bickering. → What do you need to do? → Resolve. → Continue playing. → Unresolved? → Go to time-out.

Stage 3 — Coping With Arousal

During Stage 3, the negative interaction continues and escalates. All those involved become more angered and out of control. This is the most difficult stage of anger management. Mom gets more physically tense and with increased anger, clear focused thinking is reduced. She feels more hopeless and powerless. But notice that as she continues to use her positive coping statements, she reduces her feelings of hopelessness, powerlessness, and anger. She then refocuses on resolving the discipline problem. She removes herself personally from the situation.

Stage 4 — Reflecting On the Provocation

Once the discipline situation ends, reflect on:
- What you remembered and did well.
- What skills you still need to practice.

Parents often skip this stage. If things go well, you need to praise yourself and recognize how well you are doing and how your hard work is paying off. Guilt and self-hatred often follow a discipline situation that slipped out of control. Perhaps you started out calmly and in control at Stage 1, but when your child continued to talk back, you became frustrated and resorted to yelling and name-calling. Don't overlook your positive behavior during Stage 1. Evaluate what you can do next time during Stage 3 to keep the chain short so you don't lose control or resort to name-calling. You may need to review and change or strengthen your anger management methods.

Example:

After time-out, James is prompted to apologize to Diana for pushing her and must restate the rule aloud:

James: "I'm sorry I pushed you Diana; I should have used my words and not my hands."

Mother: "And what did you want to say to Diana?"

James: "You make me mad when you take my things and I don't like it. I don't want to play with you."

Mother: "You can show her how angry you are with your words, but if you hurt her, you will be punished." (Rule and consequence restated.)

Diana: "James can go first."

Or:

James: "O.K. Set the timer, but next time I go first."

Mother: Sets timer; ignores James' last comment, recognizing that it is said as an ego defense.

In Summary: This example illustrates the importance of recognizing your *cognitive distortions*. By re-evaluating these distortions, using positive coping statements, you can refocus and reduce your anger. This is especially challenging as your child continues to argue, protest, and disobey. Knowing what discipline approach to take and staying *emotionally detached* increases your sense of control and lessens your anger.

Recognizing your current stage of anger allows you to gauge the challenge level of the situation. As you go from Stage 1 to Stage 3, you can remind yourself through positive coping statements that the situation is more difficult at Stage 3. It is even more important for you to stay calm, matter-of-fact, and to be clear about what you need to do.

TURNING "LEMON-THOUGHTS" INTO "COOL-AID"

Developing Positive, Calming, Coping Statements

You've learned the role that your negative *lemon-thoughts* play in determining how angry you become. Anger Management requires that you learn the skill of being mentally, as well as physically, relaxed. Developing and using calming coping statements will aid you in staying mentally calm during discipline. For example, at the beginning of a discipline situation, take a deep breath and say to yourself:

- *"Relax. Don't lose your cool."*
- You might also say, *"Stay relaxed. What's the problem and what do I need to do?"*
- Or, *"Don't take it personally. Stay detached."*
- Or, *"This is a parent and child matter. I have to remember that I am the parent and am in charge."*
- Or, *"Neither of us needs confrontation. My child needs direction. Remain calm."*

These coping thoughts will help you to keep your anger at a moderate level so that you can think clearly and implement the necessary discipline. Contrast the calming thoughts with the following:

You hear your kids fighting and screaming; your chest tenses. You think, *"Why can't they get along? I don't know what to do with them; they're driving me nuts! They know I have to prepare dinner and they still yell,*

'MOM!' I can't take this." These defeating thoughts can make you feel helpless and hopeless and cause you to react defensively in anger.

> **Remember: When angry thoughts race through your mind vying for verbal expression, you are less likely to focus on effective problem solving and you become a less effective disciplinarian. (Take time to listen to your relaxation CDs daily.)**

UNDERSTANDING THE PROCESS OF ANGER

STAGE 1:

Situation

You are in the kitchen preparing dinner. You need to stay by the stove and stir, so the food won't stick. You hear your kids (3- and 5-year-olds) arguing about a toy. You hear the 3-year-old scream.

Possible Antecedents

Kids playing alone longer than 20 minutes. Having difficulty resolving their problem without adult guidance. Kids are hungry. Mom is preoccupied.

Thoughts and Self-Talk

"Maybe they'll work it out. I can't let this food stick. (Hear a cry.) This happens every time! I can't ever get dinner ready without an interruption! Jason (5-years-old) is always bothering his sister."

Cognitive Distortions

Denial. Overgeneralization. Black and White Thinking.

Coping Statement

"They're only 3- and 5-year-olds. I've left them unsupervised too long. They need my help." Turn off the stove.

"Relax. You know what to do. If they resolve it, good; if not, set the timer. Stay calm. Your job is to teach them how to solve their problems and control themselves."

What the Child Learns

How to problem solve.
How to delay gratification.

Effective Discipline Approach

Mom: "What's the problem?"
Jason: "I had the truck and she took it away!"
Diana: "I had it first!"
Jason: "You put it down!"
Mom: "You both want the truck. How are you going to solve your problem so you don't have to go to time-out?"
Jason: (Holding the truck.) "Set the timer."
Mom: "Diana, you play with the truck until the bell rings, and then it's Jason's turn. You guys figured out what to do; now you don't have to go to time-out. Good job!"

STAGE 2:

Situation

Jason, feeling angrier, refuses to let Diana have truck first until the timer rings.

Possible Antecedents

Kids playing too long unsupervised. Unable to resolve conflict.

Thoughts and Self-Talk

"Why doesn't Jason just let it go? He's such a whiner and so stubborn! Who cares about the silly truck! There are other things he can play with. They never play without fighting."

Cognitive Distortions

Should Statement, Labeling.
Seeing it from your view only.
Minimizing. Black and White
Thinking. Over Generalization.

Coping Statements

"Don't label! Take a breath and relax! Both kids are having a difficult time sharing and seeing things from the other's perspective. Guarding territory is normal for their age. The rule is that they resolve 'property disputes' with the timer or both go to time-out for bickering."

Effective Discipline Approach

Mom: "You guys are still bickering. Both of you go to time-out." (Timer set.) "Jason on the pink chair, Diana on the brown chair."

Jason: "It's her fault! Now see what you've done!" (Directed to Diana.)

Mom: Ignores Jason; only concerned with Jason's and Diana's movement towards time-out locations.

What the Child Learns

1. "If I don't resolve my differences quickly, play stops and I'm put in a boring place."
Jason weighs whether he's willing to let Diana go first with the truck and avoid time-out, or continue the bickering and go to time-out.
2. "Mom doesn't tolerate escalated bickering."
3. "Mom is consistent in putting me in time-out if I keep bickering."

STAGE 3:

Situation	Possible Antecedents	Thoughts and Self-Talk
Jason refuses to go to time-out and angrily pushes his sister.	Again, playing too long unsupervised and need help resolving conflict.	*"Who does he think he's talking to! That brat! I can't believe he just did that! He needs to be pushed!"*

Cognitive Distortions	Coping Statements	Effective Discipline Approach
Personalizing. Labeling.	*"Don't take this so personally. You're losing it. Relax. You know what to do. You're the parent, teach him."*	**Mom:** "You can't push and hurt others when you're angry. We only use words to show our anger." (Diana picked up and comforted.) "Jason, go to time-out now. You have five more minutes and there is no TV tonight. If you choose to disobey, you won't play with your friends today or tomorrow."

What the Child Learns

The rule is restated regarding how to vent anger (with words not hands).
"Mom is focusing on my behavior, not who I am. Mom is in control (not me) and isn't going to back down."
Jason weighs going to time-out now or facing a more undesirable consequence (no friends).

It has been suggested by some child health care practitioners that children may instigate friction between themselves and siblings or playmates to elicit the attention and intervention of parents, caregivers, or teachers. It appeared from observing these children that they — perhaps without conscious thought — created situations hoping they would be praised and the other children involved would be scolded. One tell-tale sign: The children showed a high degree of interest in the reactions of adults monitoring their activities, rather than focusing on the activities.

To prevent or manage such incidents:

- Do not leave children unsupervised for long periods of time.
- If needed, give children help resolving conflict.

ANGER EXAMPLE

Situation

Mom is excited, anticipating a loving reunion with 5-year-old Michael when she picks him up at school. As Mom reaches out to hug and kiss him, he frowns, seems distracted and disinterested, and pulls away. Mom says, "Man, what a grouch! What's wrong with you?"

Thoughts and Self Talk

"He doesn't like me. He doesn't miss me as much as I miss him. He's so cold. What's wrong with our relationship? Why does he act like this all the time? He never cuddles like his sister."

Cognitive Distortions

Mind Reading, Emotional Reasoning, Labeling, Over Generalizing, Black and White Thinking.

Coping Statements

"Michael has his own style of interacting. Even at birth, he didn't like to cuddle. He doesn't have to meet my need to nurture him."

"I need to learn how to establish a connection with him in a way he likes. I'll try and learn how he wants to reconnect. Maybe a hug and kiss isn't what he likes. I'll ask him and/or try other things."

"He may be going through a tough time developmentally. Kindergarten has been challenging for him. There have been times in the past when he has allowed me to hug him and shown glee when he saw me."

"He's his own person, respect his style. Don't take his reaction so personally. Try to meet him on his level. Maybe he's struggling with something and will talk with me about it later."

CHAPTER 7

A STEP BEYOND "ACCENTUATING THE POSITIVE"

In prior chapters, the focus has been on changing your child's behavior using primarily *positive* means and you have learned that:

- Providing consistent praise and attention increases desired behaviors.
- *Ignoring* is one option to decrease minor negative behaviors.
- By increasing desired behaviors, negative behaviors have decreased.

Nevertheless, some negative behaviors may be more deeply ingrained and stronger discipline measures may be needed. Methods specifically designed **to decrease inappropriate behaviors,** are now introduced. In this section, you will learn:

- How to more *directly* decrease negative behaviors.
- How to provide specific, consistent consequences, including *time-out and earning privileges.*

To achieve desired behavior change you must:

- **Continue to monitor, praise, and attend to positive behaviors.**
- **Use positive methods in tandem with more punishing approaches.**

Research shows that parents often forget about providing positive praise and attention and rely more on administering punishment when addressing their children's behaviors. Punishing may seem quicker and more natural than using positive praise and attention.

However, continued use of encouraging comments will keep children motivated and keep your relationship with your child upbeat.

Privileges For *Nothing*? — That *Price* May Not Be Right!

Children typically enjoy many free positive events daily, regardless of the behavior they display. They watch favorite TV shows, talk on the 'phone, invite friends over, go to the park, go to the mall, go out for treats, drive the car, and spend special activity time with parents. As motivation to decrease negative behavior, devise a plan whereby your child *earns* these *privileges* based on demonstrating daily behaviors you consider appropriate and necessary.

For example, after school:
- Andrew usually drops his backpack on the floor in the family room.
- His Mother picks it up and reminds him that he should put it on his desk.
- Andrew ignores Mother, turns TV on and slumps on couch to enjoy his favorite show.
- Mother, irritated that Andrew does not comply, takes his backpack to his room and puts it on his desk.

Despite Andrew's undesirable behavior (dropping his backpack on the floor), he is allowed to engage in a fun activity (watching TV). Why does Andrew persist in this undesirable habit despite his Mother's reminding and scolding? **Clearly:** No effective consequence was given to teach him to behave otherwise.

An Overview: Mother's *negative attention* in the form of scolding and sighs of exasperation reinforces his habit. Andrew has learned from experience that ignoring Mom will result in her putting the backpack in the designated place. Instead of receiving a meaningful punishment, Andrew's negative behavior was followed by a positive reinforcer (watching TV).

As part of a new contract system discussed ahead of time, TV becomes a *privilege* Andrew will *earn* by first putting his backpack in the proper location (without being told). If, and only if, Andrew puts his backpack on his desk (without Mother asking), will he be allowed to watch TV. The new routine then becomes:
- Andrew walks in the house, immediately goes to his room and puts his backpack on his desk.

- Next, Mother greets and praises him for that behavior and tells him he has earned half an hour of TV.

If Andrew forgets and drops his backpack on the floor, not only has he *not* earned TV, but he is **assigned extra chores.**

No doubt your kids like receiving extras and enjoying many activities, though they do not behave as you feel they should. For example:

> By 10:00 a.m. Mary's 5-year-old son Alex had hit his sister three times, refused to come to breakfast, and had taken cookies without asking. Mother scolded him for each offense. Nevertheless, at 10:10 a.m., Alex was happily playing with his action figures as he watched his favorite TV show.

It is your responsibility to teach your kids they must first exhibit the behaviors you expect if they are to enjoy extras. If they do not exhibit the desired behaviors, assess an appropriate consequence. Then: Stick with your decision!

AN EXAMPLE OF "GRANDMA'S RULE": Earning Privileges

Grandma's Rule states: **A child must do *expected* activities before they do more *preferred* activities**. For example:
- Jeffrey must finish his homework before he can watch TV.
- Kelsey must make her bed and put her clothes away before she goes over to a friend's house.
- Jayden must mow the lawn before he goes to a movie.

Using Grandma's rule, children can be taught to perform parentally desired behaviors more often in order to receive something the children like, or to do something they want to do. Under Grandma's Rule, children should behave appropriately in order to receive *anything* special.

There is a pressing need for this generation's parents to rely on Grandma's Rule. Kids must be taught that achievement requires effort and often involves delay of gratification. Today's parents are experiencing the consequences of their *extreme overindulgence of their children*. A heavy net of woe has fallen over the family unit as parents are forcefully reminded of the following:

. . . for whatever a man sows, that he will also reap. (Galatians 6:7)

Parents are often slow in acknowledging what should be evident initially: The more material possessions kids acquire, the more they desire. Grandma might say: **"Children today suffer from a malady called the *want-itis*, and the cure is applications of Grandma's Rule."** For instance: *Many parents notice that new acquisitions may cause their kids to experience fleeting feelings of satisfaction; however, almost before sales tags are removed from an item, their kids lose interest and are pleading for, and usually get, the next highly advertised "must have."*

Parents should have no difficulty understanding the roots of their children's attitude of expecting everything with nothing given in return: Never have parents been so focused on appeasing their kids' every wish and whim *and* had the money to do so! This particular domain of *want it, need it, got-to-have-it-now* once was inhabited mostly by spoiled teens. Now, age is a non-factor: Children of all ages often exhibit an air of entitlement and belief that instant gratification is their due. One author refers to this generation as being the most narcissistic *ever*.

Parental permissiveness brought about this circular situation of: *They want, I give; they want, I give.* The other side of that coin, from their children's viewpoint, is: *I want, I get; I want, I get.* Anxious to provide their children with every advantage, today's parents act with loving intentions which often prove detrimental: The backlash of those actions has negatively affected our children's future. Parents are facing the fact that they have created an unrealistic world for their children. The result: A generation of children who expect much, give little, and rarely choose to delay gratification long enough to achieve excellence.

It is imperative that parents set limits if their children are to thrive in the world beyond the comfort zone of their home and family.

Think for a moment about your children's reaction to the word "No." A drama coach could not coax a more varied range of emotions as the word falls upon their ears: Disbelief, wheedling, tears, anger, histrionics, pouting and, probably, momentary threats of "You'll be sorry." *After you tell your child "No," end the conversation. Do not reply to their prolonged entreaties with variations of:*

- "I said, no!"
- "Didn't you hear me say, no?"
- "Even if you keep asking, the answer is still, no."
- "How many times do I have to tell you the answer is, no?"

The answer to the last question is: Until you make your children understand that "No" means "No," and stop further conversation about the subject. Negative reinforcement is still reinforcement! Follow any form of talking back or disobedience with point or privilege loss.

Thinking Points:

- Have you considered the behavior you are modeling for your children?
- Do your spending habits influence and fuel your children's constant demands?

As an alternative to *revoking* privileges, have your children *earn* their privileges. First, determine what things or activities your children especially enjoy, look forward to or find motivating. Then, insist they behave appropriately to access these privileges. At a minimum, children should:

- Follow household rules devised by parents, including doing chores, completing homework, and keeping curfews.
- Respect and obey their parents and authority figures.
- Respect the rights of others.
- Perform commensurate to their ability in school and elsewhere.

Using Charts: "Yes. No! Well, Maybe . . ."

For many parents, using charts to change behavior seems time consuming. However, keeping a chart is an effective tool for achieving behavior change. When you record your behavior, for example, it causes you to turn inward, focus on, and observe yourself. This self-monitoring procedure is a step to achieving behavior change. Parents often ask, "I know my older children understand, but does my young child really understand what the chart means?" The kids do not have to understand charting; the chart's main function is to aid parents.

The chart acts as a stimulus, reminding both you and your child how things are changing. Seeing the chart helps the parent remember what behaviors they are monitoring. The tallies tell both parent and child how much behavior change is occurring, and whether the child is still motivated by the program. When you verbally define the observed behavior ("You came when I called. Great job! That's a plus point!"), and mark the chart, your child sees that you are serious about making changes.

Children can also see:

- That you are consistent in noticing whether their desired behavior occurred.
- That you are consistent in implementing appropriate consequences.

Finally, the chart is useful in reducing confusion and disagreement over whether certain behaviors occurred, points were earned or back up reinforcers or punishers should be given.

In Summary: Though not necessary to the overall success of effecting change in behaviors, charting helps you develop the habit of monitoring, attending to, and praising your child's positive behaviors. The chart also shows your child that preplanned consequences are in place for negative behaviors.

Using Charts: "Okay, I'll Give It A Try."

Use more punishing methods like point loss and time-out only if needed. Always *first* chart and praise the desired positive behavior. That may result in the change you want without any form of punishment. Next, your child earns privileges contingent upon a specified number of tally marks for positive behavior. If the rate of negative behavior remains too high, use a chart and record both positive and negative behaviors. Positive tallies are then subtracted from negative tallies. *Designated privileges are earned only if more positive than negative behaviors occurred.*

If some negative behaviors still persist, combine the chart with time-out. Each time the child goes into time-out, points are lost for the negative behavior as well. Keep focusing on positive behaviors and keep praising. If you marked down each time you praised your child or said anything positive to any family member, you probably noticed that you praised more than before you used the chart. You may have noticed that your child's positive behaviors increased and the family atmosphere is more pleasant.

Reminder: *Research shows the more positives we give out, the more positives we receive.*

"High-Five" Your Child's Positive Behavior With Points!

Earlier, you praised and marked a tally each time a positive behavior occurred. Then you listed privileges your child now must earn based on their behavior. They must behave the way you expect them to, in order to enjoy previously taken-for-granted extras. They must *earn* their daily privileges. Their behavior does not have to be perfect for them to have the extras they enjoy, but the percentage of their negative behavior (relative to their positive behavior) must be reasonably low.

You may choose to chart one or two behaviors at a time. As these behaviors are changed, you can then address another behavior. If you choose to chart, you may want to follow these five simple steps:

Step 1: List negative behaviors you want to decrease. Then, list positive behaviors you want to increase.

Step 2: Arrange the behaviors beginning with those you want to change first.

Step 3: List privileges your child currently receives free.

Step 4: Develop a simple contract with your child: Your child exhibits desired behaviors and receives a given number of points to be used to earn the once free privileges. You are communicating to your child that in order for them to have "extras" they have to follow rules you set and exhibit behaviors you expect. A simple contract might be on curfew limits. For instance:

> If Bryce is five minutes late, he will lose an hour next week (be home by 10:00 p.m. instead of 11:00 p.m.). If he is 10 minutes late, he will lose two hours (be home by 9:00 p.m. next week). If he is 15 minutes (or more) late, he will not be allowed to go out next Saturday.

Step 5: The challenge will be: Whether you will follow-through with the consequences when faced with protests and verbal or physical childish outbursts. List desired child behaviors, the number of points earned and the privileges for which the points may be traded. Having a plan before expected outbursts or negative behaviors occur defuses your anger and gives the child the consistency he needs.

List of Child's Privileges

1.
2.
3.
4.
5.
6.
7.
8.
9.
10.

"Keeping Count: One, Two, Three . . ."

Put rules in place to help children rack up those positive points! For instance, Pat will have to "talk respectfully" five times and "do what she's asked" 10 times from 6:30 a.m. to 8:00 a.m. in order to "earn the right to watch TV." In the same daily timeframe, she must exhibit these behaviors 15 times to play with a friend after school and 30 times to go to the movies. (This may take more than one day.)

Preschoolers require immediate feedback. They also need to have their slate wiped clean more often or they will quickly become discouraged. For children 15 months to three years, make the interval for earning privileges very short. This allows the child to practice and learn the desired behavior and experience success.

Example:

Child: Katie, 3-years-old.
Behavior to be decreased: Temper tantrums (yelling, crying, flailing) when told "No."
Behavior to be increased: Do immediately what she is told.
Consequence: During the first week, Katie must earn five points to watch a favorite TV show at 9:00 a.m. She can earn a point only by accepting "No" and doing what she's told without tantrums. Also, for every tantrum reaction, Katie is placed immediately in time-out for three minutes. To increase

feelings of success, Mother begins by asking Katie to do things she knows she will probably do. Thus, at first, Katie earns her points easily and quickly.

Mother: "Katie, hand Mommy that bowl, please."
Katie: Hands bowl to Mother.
Mother: "Oh! You did what I asked immediately, Katie. That's a point!"

Mother will continue for a time to make it easy for Katie to earn points and experience encouragement for changing her behavior. Eventually, Katie will be expected to demonstrate immediate obedience to more challenging commands. That is, Mother will use *shaping* to teach Katie to accept "No" and to immediately do what she is asked.

"Counting Down: Three, Two, One . . ."

Your kids will soon learn negative behaviors can *gobble up* their hard earned positive points. If your child's negative behaviors do not decrease after one or two weeks through use of a positive point system, begin taking away points for the negative behaviors. You can then derive a *grand total* of points which will be used to determine which, if any, privileges have been earned. To enjoy extras as previously discussed, your child will need to exhibit more positive than negative behaviors. The goal is for the child to learn and exhibit appropriate behavior which becomes habit, making lists and charts unnecessary.

CHARTS: Stepping Stones Or Stumbling Blocks?

"My Child Gets Upset When He Loses Points."

Children may react negatively or become very upset when points are taken away. Using primarily a positive point system may be more effective if your child seems to overreact to points being taken away. However, if their negative behavior does not decrease, eventually you may have to take points away. Some children's egos and self-esteem may be so fragile that taking points away is too much for them. Try to determine why they are so sensitive to negative feedback. Several possible *antecedents* (factors influencing your child's behavior) should be explored:

- Do you inadvertently communicate to your child that mistakes are not okay?
- Perhaps your child experiences negative feedback as parental rejection.
- Maybe your child has heard mostly negative comments if he misbehaves a lot.
- Are your standards too high?

"My Child Has Lost Interest In Charts And Points."

"And, frankly, so have I." Don't use a chart system if you find it's too complicated (too many behaviors to list, points to dole out, and consequences to put in place). If you do choose to use a chart, keep it simple and keep in mind that the chart will be phased out. That is, you will stop using it when you reach the desired results (usually within a few weeks).

"I Don't Have Time To Keep A Chart!"

Life seems so stressful at times; often both parents are working and adding one more thing to your to-do list can overwhelm you. If that is the case, do not keep a chart. Later, if you feel charting may help: Make a simple chart.

"How Do I Make My Kids Earn Something They Used To Get Free?"

If you feel intimidated about *making* your children obey, consider that tacitly you may have given your children authority to do as they please. Perhaps this is an indication that you have allowed your children to control decisions that should be parental decisions. Your children will not be happy having to earn privileges they previously got for free. *However, you are taking a giant step toward making your children accountable and responsible for their behavior. Whether your children are happy about your decision should not be a priority.*

"How Can I Monitor and Chart All My Children At Once?"

Remember: Keep the program simple! If it seems too

overwhelming, continue to monitor, but do not chart. However, let each child know you are monitoring them. Devise a system that suits your schedule and purposes.

In Review:

1. Children must be trained by parents to behave appropriately.
2. Use praise every time positive behaviors occur.
3. Deduct a point and/or put the child in time-out each time negative behaviors occur.
4. Privileges are earned based on the total number of points received for positive behaviors.
5. To increase follow-through, place several timers at various spots around the house and one in the car.

A FIVE POINT SUMMARY OF ACP

- **First**, *always* **start with positive procedures:** use *positive means alone* (preferably with charting) to change your child's behavior. As the positive child behaviors increase, the negative behaviors will decrease. (Be sure to give large doses of love, encouragement, and attention daily!)
- **Second**, if positive praise and attention fail to yield the results you desire then have your child *earn privileges using positive, but not negative, points* on a chart.
- **Third, move on to more punishing procedures** if some problem behaviors still persist. Children *earn privileges based on positive minus negative points* recorded on the chart.
- **Fourth**, if the problem behaviors continue to decrease, but still not enough, then *combine the positive/negative point chart system of privileges earned with time-out.*
- **Fifth**, once you have attained the desired rate of positive behavior, *phase out point system and time-out.* Thereafter, use the point system and/or time-out as needed.

When the identified problem behaviors have been adequately reduced, you might use an abbreviated chart just with positive tallies for appropriate behavior. These tallies continue to be used for daily privileges and, for older kids, they might be cashed in for money.

Part of the money could go toward paying for their extra-curricular activities. *Discuss beforehand if the expenditure of the money is at their sole discretion or involves parental input.*

LET'S PULL IT ALL TOGETHER!

Notice in the example below how 8-year-old Molly was taught by her Mother to talk with respect, using points on a chart and time-out. Consequences for talking back during discipline had been discussed with her previously and remained in place should future slips occur.

If a disrespectful gesture or remark was minor (sarcastic *"Okay!"*), Molly was simply asked to rephrase it respectfully. Mother said, "Talk with respect, Molly." Molly repeated, "Okay, Mom" (in a proper tone). Another option was: Mother told Molly the expected rephrase and Molly repeated it. For example, Mother said "Okay, Mom" (in a proper tone), and Molly repeated, "Okay, Mom" (in a proper tone).

If the disrespect was more serious (Molly said, "Why can't *you* do it, are you lazy?"), Molly was told to go to time-out and that she lost the privilege of friends coming over that day. After time-out, she was told to rephrase the remark and that she was not allowed to express her thoughts to her parents in a disrespectful way.

Teaching your child appropriate behavior will not squelch your child's feelings and ability to express anger. Molly needs to express her negative feelings to her Mother *respectfully*. Empathy can be expressed, but *discussion of feelings should be scheduled after the discipline.*

Mother: "Molly, do the dishes now."
Molly: "It's not fair! Why do *I* always have to do the dishes?"
Mother: "That's a point off your chart for talking back." (Mother walks out of the room and waits to see if Molly starts doing the dishes.)

If Molly begins the dishes, she is praised. If she does not, she is *immediately* sent to time-out and/or is told to write sentences

("I will obey my Mother without talking back."). Further, Molly loses points off her chart. After the incident is over, Mother communicates empathy but restates that talking back is not tolerated.

Mother: "It's not easy when I tell you what to do, but that's how we get things done in our family. Dad and I are the ones who decide who does what and when. Sometimes it seems unfair to you, *but I expect you to do what we say without talking back. After you do what we ask, then we are willing to hear about your feelings.*"

At this point Molly shares her feelings respectfully.

STOP ARGUMENTS FROM GOING ON AND ON . . . *AND ON*

Notice in the above example that Molly's feelings are acknowledged and Mother is empathetic. However, the parents' expectation of compliance to commands is restated, as is the rule that arguing or further discussion will not be tolerated. Notice also the message Mother communicated in her interaction with Molly: **Parents are identified as the leaders and authority figures in the home.** While Mother acknowledges that Molly does not like what she is being told to do, the time spent discussing the issue is short.

The chain of interaction for the above example is kept short: Mom → Molly → Mom (period!). Negative arguments do not escalate and Molly is prevented from becoming more disrespectful. Also, Mom does not resort to yelling or other means of stopping Molly's rude comments. Mother is aware she is *in control of* all desired present and future privileges. She feels strong and calm.

The General Rule Should Be: *No Discussions During Discipline.*

Sticking with the rule of **no discussions during discipline or when a command is given** will greatly reduce the length of the negative chain of interaction (and reduce your anger). Kids' disrespectful back-talk is one of the most frequent triggers of parental anger. There are times when parents should have discussion with their children about compromise and negotiation concerning discipline. However, make it clear parents will decide ahead of time which issues are open to negotiation. Too many families get into debates over such minor commands as, "Come in now," "It's time for bed," or "I want you to do the dishes." If there is a disagreement, let your child know you heard them and that they can write about it to discuss later or bring it up in the next family meeting. But, for now, the discussion is over.

Always be open to your child's views and try to understand their desires and needs. After consideration, however, parental decisions should be based on the good of the child and the good of the family. *There are many decisions that should not be left up to a child. Nevertheless, you can count on them to try and convince you otherwise!* Children develop self-control and respect for authority if they have been taught to obey parents, and understand parents have the final say in family decisions. There are ample opportunities to help your child develop independent thinking and the ability to disagree, discuss topics, and negotiate in an appropriate manner. Parents can create and take advantage of such opportunities.

Discussions about rewards or consequences should also take place when discipline is NOT the issue. For instance, assuming you want your children to make decisions or offer suggestions, you might ask questions as follows:

- "Do you want popsicles after lunch or dinner?"
- "How do you think we should spend our time today?"
- "When do you think you should do your homework?"
- "What ideas do you have for splitting chores?"
- "What time do you think your curfew should be?"

"Shape Up" Positive Behaviors — "Ship Out" Negative Behaviors!

Some behavior changes need to be broken down into small steps called ***shaping***. For example, parents often say, "I can't get my child to go to time-out," or "Once they are there, they leave." For children between the ages of two- and five-years-old, you might break down achieving the desired behavior of *going to and staying in time-out* into the following steps:

1. Explain in simple terms the purpose of time-out and how it works. For example: "Mommy wants to stop yelling so much when you disobey me. So, from now on, when I ask you to pick up your toys or come to me and you don't do

it right away, you're going to have to sit on this chair. I'm going to set the timer and you have to sit there until the bell rings."

2. Demonstrate and have child practice (role-play).

3. If your child adamantly refuses to go to the chair, have them sit where they are, set the timer, and ding it after about 10 to 20 seconds.

4. The next time the child has to go to time-out, wait until they at least touch the chair, and then ding the timer after 10 to 20 seconds.

5. The next time, wait for your child to sit on the chair, and wait a little longer before you ding the timer (about 1 minute).

6. Finally, you will wait until the child is sitting down on the chair facing the wall for three minutes.

7. The next step involves teaching your child to sit quietly. Eventually, when you instruct your child to go to time-out, they will go on their own and sit quietly until the bell rings for the designated time.

In Summary: *Shaping* reinforces approximations to the desired behavior. Gradually, expect the child to exhibit more of the behavior before you provide the consequence. Eventually, the child demonstrates the exact behavior or chain of behaviors before receiving the consequences. During the beginning stages, monitor and prompt your child.

Shaping can be used to teach young toddlers to pick up their toys, by offering a lot of help at first, then gradually turning most of the task over to them. At first, they receive praise while being assisted, and then gradually praise follows only after *they* put more and more toys away.

Using *shaping* is also an effective way to teach your preschooler to dress themselves. At first you do most of the dressing, praising them for cooperation and for helping you. Next, you have the child put their underwear on and praise them. Continue to finish dressing them. The next day, after child puts on underwear, hand child socks to put on and praise child. Similarly, give them the top and pants or skirt or dress to finish the clothing sequence, praising them as they complete each step.

Eventually, you will guide them only verbally as they self-dress: When the child puts on their underwear, praise; then the top, praise, etc. In future, when it is time to dress, you will announce, "Come and get dressed" and go with them to the room where they dress. Watch and exhibit delight as they get dressed independently. You will intermittently praise certain steps, eventually praising only at the end with, "Great job!" or "Boy, you can dress yourself!"

A common mistake made by parents is to tell young children to get dressed without the parent's assistance. Parents often believe if the young child knows how to dress themselves, they should do so without the parent present. Young children are easily distracted and easily frustrated; parents need to supervise.

Thinking Point: Frequently, devise ways to encourage your children to take risks and to develop problem solving skills. Take time to ask your children *why* questions and encourage their *why* questions.

Examples:
- "Why do you think they put water in this can of corn?"
- "Why do we need to put oil in the pan first when we prepare food or pop corn?"
- "Why does popcorn pop?"
- "Why does this strawberry gelatin quiver and shake?"
- "Why does milk spoil if it's in the refrigerator?"
- "Why does ice-cream melt?"

Jan: "Why are the car windows wet and foggy in the morning?"

Mom: "That's an interesting question. Why do you think?"

Jan: "I don't know. Just tell me."

Mom: "You guess and then I will. Later, we can look it up in the encyclopedia and check our guesses."

Note that the focus isn't on *right* or *wrong* answers, but on checking the guesses.

"FIVE EASY STEPS: CONTROL ANGER BY RELAXING"

Many parents would agree that anything involving relaxing

while simultaneously accomplishing something sounds like a plan worth exploring!

You can learn to relax, first in response to an event that makes you angry and then to events that make you progressively angrier. In clinical terms this is labeled: Systematic Desensitization to Anger Provoking Events. (An Anger Hierarchy form is provided in Chapter 2 if you choose to try this method of relaxation.)

Step 1. Rate your current level of tension and anxiety from 0 to 10 (least to most).

Step 2. Listen to progressive relaxation CDs and relax completely, physically and mentally.

Step 3. Imagine the first event on your anger hierarchy. Feel the physical and mental upset, tenseness, and anger envelop you. Notice anger provoking self-statements such as, "I can't stand this!" "This kid is driving me crazy!"

Step 4. Give yourself the command to relax your whole body and use your anger coping statements such as "Breathe deeply and relax." "I can handle this." "It's okay. If it doesn't go perfectly, I'll do better next time."

Step 5. Rate your anger level 0-10 again. If your rating exceeds 3, repeat Steps 1 to 5. Once your rating is at 0 or 1, go on to the next item on the hierarchy and repeat Steps 1 to 5.

Practicing systematic desensitization allows you to physically and mentally rehearse how to control your anger and relax when facing progressively challenging anger situations.

WHAT *YOU* "SAID" VERSUS WHAT *THEY* "HEARD"

Effective communication is another important antecedent to your child's behavior. What you say and *how you say it* directly influences how your child will respond. Giving your child a command to do something is a different form of communication than inviting an open discussion on a topic. Parents must be clear: Is the topic open for discussion or a command to be obeyed?

In addition to teaching children to obey, parents must teach and model effective, respectful communication skills. Listen to your kids, reflect what you heard them say and encourage them to share their opinions. This lays the foundation for a close lifetime relationship. Many parents either never build, or they destroy, lines of communication with their children. Often, parents are baffled as to why their kids do not open up and share, when the only impediment may be lack of *effective* communication. **Three requirements for effective communication are:**

- **A sender**
- **A receiver**
- **A concise message clearly understood**

"Let's Hear It One More Time . . ." — Giving Feedback

This consists of letting the person talking (the sender) know what you (the receiver) heard the sender say. There are two main types of reflective feedback:

1. Literal Reflection. You (the receiver) tell the speaker exactly what you heard.

Example: Mom: "Amy, I'd like you to clean the bathroom now."

Amy (8-years-old): "I've been cleaning all morning and now I can't play with my friends. This isn't fair."

Mom: "You've been cleaning all morning long and now you want to play with your friends? You don't think this work schedule is fair."

Amy: "Yeah!"

2. Inferential Reflection. The receiver tries to reflect the thoughts and feelings behind the message.

Example: Mom: "Sounds like you're feeling pretty frustrated that I have another chore for you to do. You feel as if you've waited a long time to play."

Amy: "Yeah and it's not fair."

Mom: "It doesn't seem fair to you."

Mom, the receiver, has provided Amy, the sender, an opportunity to correct the impression of how she's feeling.

The challenge of inferential feedback is to reflect what the speaker seems to be thinking and feeling. The listener must try to understand and relate the sender's viewpoint. Taking the perspective of an angry child may not be easy, but it reduces the angry feelings of both you and your child. Taking time to listen carefully and reflect back what you heard does not mean that you agree with your child or that you intend to do what they want.

Continuing with the example:

Mom: "I understand how you feel Amy. You still must clean the bathroom before you go out."

Amy: "Mom!!!!"

Mom: "I'm sorry. Sometimes it's not easy to do what Dad and I say. But I expect you to obey. If you choose to argue with me now, you'll still have to clean the bathroom, but you won't be allowed to play after you complete your chore."

In this example, Mother "heard" and reflected Amy's thoughts and feelings. Note three things in this example:

- **First**, Mom and Dad ultimately decide the outcome. If Mom has no objections if Amy cleans the bathroom at a later time, she might say, "Okay, you can play first and clean up at 6:30 p.m."
- **Second**, Mom reminds Amy of the rule: Once Amy's point of view is heard and Mom makes her decision, no more debate is allowed.
- **Third**, if Amy chooses to continue debating (arguing, protesting), she will still have to do the chore but will forfeit playtime.

This structured form of communication increases the likelihood that the chain of negative interaction will stay short. Keeping the discipline chain of interaction short (discussion → decision → consequences for arguing), reduces parents' feelings of frustration and loss of control; this also reduces the likelihood of escalating parental anger.

Children learn that their views are respected, but parents and other authority figures ultimately make certain decisions for them. Listening to and validating your child's thoughts and feelings models respectfulness. Punishing prolonged discussion or arguing teaches children:

- Self-control (*I don't always get what I want. If I keep arguing, I'll be worse off.*)
- Delay of gratification (*I have to wait and do my chores before I have fun and play.*)
- Respect for authority (*What Mom says goes.*)

"That's What — *Or Not What* — I Thought You Said."

The purpose of giving and receiving feedback is to check out what we thought the person said.

This is important because:

- We often make erroneous assumptions about what others meant by their words.
- Feedback allows us to share our observations and to tell others how their behavior affects us.

FIVE DIRECTIVES NECESSARY TO GIVE AND RECEIVE EFFECTIVE FEEDBACK

1.   **Be Specific**

2.   **Be Descriptive**

Describe what you saw rather than making negative comments, evaluations, or judgments. For instance, you might say, "Jumping on the bed is not allowed," rather than, "You're just showing off." Or, "You do that just to get attention." Or, "That was a stupid move." Such negative comments are put-downs that make the child defensive, attack their self-esteem, provide negative attention, and do not address the behavior or expected change.

3.   **Focus On The Behavior That You See, Not The Child's Intention**

For example, say "You're jumping off the top bunk," versus "You're trying to make me mad." State and describe the specific behavior you want changed. "The rule is no jumping on the bed."

4.   **Be Empathetic**

Try to *walk* in your child's shoes and be sensitive to their feelings and consider how he might hear your feedback. (Remember how you felt during discipline?) For example, you might say, "You are a brave jumper and it looks like you have fun jumping from a high place. However, I'm afraid you might get hurt. In our house, furniture isn't for play. The rule is no jumping from the top bunk."

5.   **Explain the Problem**

Let the child know how the behavior affects you and/or why you see it as a problem. For example, Mom says to Megan, "I've asked you not to wear my good shoes outside while you're playing. When you do, I feel like you don't care about my things."

In Review:

- Children can — and should — be given ample opportunities daily to problem-solve and make decisions regarding their life.
- Their feelings and views about the family and discipline can be expressed during family meetings or other non-discipline situations.
- Some decisions are reserved for parents. Parents have the authority to make decisions based on what is best for the child, the parents, and the family.

Examples Of Daily Decisions Children Can Make:

1. What to wear to school (from pre-approved categories).
2. How to wear their hair (from pre-approved categories).
3. How to spend their free time (within reason).
4. How to prioritize their homework.
5. What items they will buy with their "spending" money (from pre-approved categories).
6. What vegetable to have for dinner.
7. What kind of sandwich and/or snacks they would choose for their lunch.
8. What library books they want to choose (monitored by parent).
9. What gift they want to buy friends, siblings, parents (within reason).
10. How they will construct a project.
11. Do they prefer a flat or higher pillow to sleep on?
12. How to decorate their room (with your approval).

CHAPTER 8

"IT'S ABOUT TIME . . ."

ALMOST EVERYTHING IS ABOUT *TIME*

Often, the word *time* is said in exasperation: "Well, it's about *time!*" Or, in a harried tone: "There's never enough *time*." Or, in a relieved tone: "Just in *time*." **This chapter, however, discusses time in another sense: Time-Out — an effective way to discipline your children if properly and consistently used.**

TIME-OUT: It Does Work!

As a mild form of punishment, time-out is generally used with toddlers and children up to about eight-years-old. *Time-out refers to removing a child from all things that are reinforcing*. When misbehavior occurs, the child is immediately sent to a chair facing the wall, or placed in another boring place, for approximately 3-to-5 minutes. Negative behaviors are identified *beforehand* so both parent and child know what behaviors will merit a time-out.

Research shows that time-out, properly used, is effective in reducing *high frequency negative* behaviors such as hitting, teasing, talking back, and whining. Time-out would not be appropriate for less frequent behaviors such as stealing and lying. Time-out should become part of your behavior change routine only if using positive strategies alone have failed to yield the desired result. Remember: Punishment alone will not yield the desired results. *Positive praise and attention must be firmly established for time-out to be effective.* Time-out can also be combined with a chart system to further reduce persistent negative behavior. (This is discussed further below.)

TIME-OUT: Commonly Asked Questions

"How Does It Work?"

Consider the following example: Mother wants to eliminate Madison's whining behavior by combining time-out with the chart system. Some success is achieved when Mother uses only positive praise and attention if Madison speaks in a clear voice. Nevertheless, Madison still whines when she does not get her way. With time-out, when Madison whines, "Why can't I keep watching TV?" Mother immediately sends her to the time-out chair. Mother says, "You're whining, go to the chair."

Note: Mother does *not* provide negative attention such as, "Why do you always have to whine? I can't stand that sound! You're getting too big for that now, stop it!" Nor does Mother answer Madison's whiney question. The discipline interaction sequence is short, calm, and matter-of-fact: Child whines. → Child is sent to Time-Out. → Bell rings. → Child is told to repeat her former words in a non-whining voice. → Mother praises child for appropriate tone and words and decides whether or not to honor the original request.

To increase your consistency in using time-out, keep a chair and a kitchen timer in place in a boring part of the house. Time-out can take place anywhere that is basically free of distractions (facing the wall in a store, restaurant, or bathroom). Research shows the optimal time spent on the chair is between 3-to-5 minutes per session.

When your child misbehaves and a time-out is assessed, calmly name the infraction and use the following sequence as a guide:

Mother says to 6-year-old Sean, "Sean, you didn't come when I called. Go to the chair (or time-out)."

Set the timer for three minutes.

Sean goes to time-out until bell rings.

Mother says, "Now, come here please."

Sean comes within three seconds.

Mother verbally praises Sean and marks a positive point on his chart. She then asks if Sean would like her to read him a story.

This is the ideal situation: Training your child to go to time-out properly may take several days. *Shaping* can be used to teach time-out to a strong-willed child who resists going anywhere near the chair. With *shaping*, the child gradually demonstrates the desired behavior. Assume you tell your daughter to go to time-out for not coming when asked. She starts to protest and cry and just lies on the floor. Allow her to stay on the floor and ding the timer after just 30 seconds and announce that time-out is over.

The next time she is sent to the chair, require that she at least touch the chair before you ding the timer and then announce, "Time-out is over." The third time she is sent to the chair, do not ding the timer until part of her body is on the chair. Gradually, expect more and more of your child's body to be on the chair before you ding the timer. Eventually, your child must sit down completely on the chair and face the wall for the full designated time.

Combining the chart system with time-out also allows your child to earn or lose points for time-out behavior. For example, in the beginning stages of training positive points can be earned for going to and completing time-out properly. Points can be lost for refusing to respond immediately, or for knocking items over or shoving, pushing or kicking items on the way, etc. Since *all* privileges require earning more positive than negative points, this is a good way to motivate your child to complete the time-out process properly.

"How Do I Explain Time-Out To My Child?"

You might present the time-out formula to your child as follows: To 7-year-old Leslie, Father says:

> "Leslie, you and I have both been working hard to change some of our negative behaviors. I'm keeping a chart on myself so that I remember to say nice things to you and Mommy. Your chart this week shows that you are putting your clothes in the hamper, and we usually don't have to remind you. That's been great! (She earns points only if she puts clothes in the hamper on her own.)
>
> "I'm still concerned with the sassy tone and words you use sometimes when I ask you to do something. After lunch today, I asked you whether you had enough to eat and you said, 'Well, duh!' That sounds disrespectful and it's not acceptable in our family. We want to help you learn to talk to Mom and Dad respectfully. So, each time you forget and talk with disrespect, you will be sent to time-out."

Focus on behaviors your child needs to learn and not endurable traits. Instead of telling your child, "You have a smart mouth," say, "I'm going to put a minus point on your chart for disrespectful talk and you have to go to time-out. That means you have to go to the pink chair facing the wall in our hallway. I will set a timer for six minutes. You have to stay in the chair without talking or playing until the timer dings, like this." (Demonstrate.) "Let's practice so you understand."

If a child does not want to practice, continue explaining how time-out works. Adapt the explanation to your child's age.

To Summarize:

- Specifically label the negative behavior (identified ahead of time as punishable by time-out). Say, "That's disrespectful talk."
- Then say, "Go to the chair," or "Go to time-out."
- Child goes to time-out within 3-to-5 seconds of the command.
- Timer is set and dings when time is up.
- Reissue the command or have child readdress offensive behavior or speech: "Say it over in a respectful tone."
- Child complies.
- Praise your child for correct behavior and say something positive to them: "That tone of voice makes me feel as if you have respect for me; makes me feel loved."

"Where Should Time-Out Take Place?"

Time-out should take place in a boring setting, where all reinforcing stimuli are removed. There should not be any TV, music, people to talk to, and nothing to see that might be entertaining or pleasurable to look at. **Time-out is, by definition, the absence of all reinforcement.** Typical time-out settings include: Placing a straight-back chair facing a blank wall, perhaps in a hallway, at the bottom of a stairway, or in the bathroom. The time-out chair should be as far away from TV and family activity as possible.

Generally, your child's bedroom is not an ideal place for time-out. Often there are many reinforcing activities in a child's bedroom, such as games, toys, books, or Nintendo which provide opportunities for fun. On the other hand, if your child does not like to be sent to their bedroom, then sending them there would be punishment, thereby decreasing their negative behavior. You can determine whether an event is experienced as punishment by whether or not the behavior decreases when it is followed by that event.

"How Long Should My Child Stay In Time-Out?"

A general rule for length of time-out periods is one minute/year-old. (Thus, a 5-year-old will stay in time-out five minutes.) Research indicates that keeping a child in time-out longer than 3-to-5 minutes is no more effective. When you restrict children to their room for extended periods — a day or more — additional problems may occur. What action do you take, for example, when another negative behavior occurs while they already are grounded for the day? All privileges have already been taken away. By mid-day, the grounded child may show positive behaviors and you might be tempted to end the restriction early.

Be aware that long-term grounding can lead to inconsistent punishment. Parents may feel they also are being punished since they have to alter their plans to monitor the grounded child. Dealing with each negative behavior as it occurs teaches the child what they did incorrectly ("You didn't come when I called. Go to the chair."). After time-out, the command is reissued, giving them another chance to *do it right* and receive praise and positive points. With time-out and charting, the problem is identified, punished, and you move on. You and your child can resume your relationship instead of harboring mutual anger and resentment.

"What If My Child Refuses To Go To Time-Out?"

This is a common occurrence, especially with young children. For that reason, when you explain how time-out works, be sure to include the following: "Let's say that you don't go to time-out when I tell you. You say, 'No! I'm not going.' We're not going to carry you or chase you. For every minute you don't go to the chair, that's another minute in time-out. If five minutes pass and you still have not gone to the chair, your bike gets locked up that day." *Prearrange a consequence that has meaning to the child for non-compliance to time-out.* Children can also be told ahead of time that refusal to go to time-out can result in point loss which will adversely affect privileges to be earned. When your child is first learning to go to time-out, give positive points when they go immediately, or when they improve in compliance each time they are sent to time-out. Eventually, these incentives will be withdrawn.

You might also keep track of the frequency of time-outs and announce ahead of time the consequence for having too many time-outs for a designated period of time. For example: Going to time-out three times before noon means losing a major thing they value (TV and phone privileges, friends over, etc.). Alternatively, after so many time-outs, you can assign a major undesirable chore (clean the bathroom, straighten closets, sweep the porch, etc.). Children may soon choose time-out over the loss of a meaningful privilege they enjoy daily.

This procedure communicates to the child that they have a choice: the chair or a bigger consequence. Leave the choice to them: Stay clear in your mind that you will implement the consequences. Also, continue providing consistent positive praise and attention to build a close, intimate relationship with your child. Most kids want to maintain that positive connection. If you are consistent in following through with consequences, your kids will know you mean what you say and they will obey the first time more often. Parents who are the most effective disciplinarians have *credibility*: Their kids know they will backup their decisions. To minimize conflict, leave the room while kids choose to obey or to accept a punishment.

"What If My Child Yells In Time-Out?"

At first, moderate out of control behavior should be ignored. In time, you will expect that, as the bell rings, your child will show self-control before they leave time-out. Normal crying and verbal complaining should be ignored. Children are told ahead of time that they are not allowed to damage anything (kick the wall or throw a toy), and if they do so, time-out will be extended and they will lose designated privileges. Remind them once of consequences if they engage in destructive behavior (kick the wall, or throw a toy). Follow-through is imperative. Initially, positive points can be earned for improving their behavior with each trip to time-out.

"What If My Toddler Keeps Getting Off The Time-Out Chair?"

This is not unusual, especially for strong-willed children. Keep in mind points are lost for not going to time-out properly; this makes it harder for the child to garner enough points for desired privileges. "But how will my toddler understand they are losing points for not going?" When you tell them that access to a favorite toy or activity is not possible because they didn't go to the time-out chair when asked, it should not take too long for them to make the connection. Rather than struggling to get the child to stay on the chair, remove points and do not give them access to desired privileges until *they choose* to obey.

At some point they will ask for a privilege; for example: "Can I go over to Sage's house?" You will reply, "Yes, as soon as you learn to *stay* in the time-out chair." An opportunity to go to time-out will be available the next time they refuse to follow your command or behave inappropriately. If they go immediately and stay in time-out the next time you instruct them to, the opportunity to access privileges is available again. Remember, if you have consistently employed positive praise and attention for appropriate behavior and trained the child to earn their privileges via the point system — your children should have developed habits of compliance. And, the probability that they will go to and stay in time-out when told is greatly increased.

To summarize: There will be ample opportunities to teach the child the consequences of *not* going to time-out. If you are consistent, your toddler will quickly learn that they get *nothing* pleasurable until they learn to sit on the chair and stay there. For children under five or six, you might put favorite toys out of reach. When they wake up the next morning, have them *earn* access to these privileges (toys to play with) *only after* successful accumulation of positive points for doing time-out properly.

"What If My Child Leaves The Time-Out Area?"

The same procedure is followed as discussed above. Again, do not get into a power struggle with the child. Use the anger control techniques and strategies you have learned. Stay detached. Label the inappropriate behavior and state the specific consequence. ("You got off the chair, that's another minute (up to five or so minutes) and point lost. If you do it again you lose another point and won't be able to earn 'X'.") *Implement the consequence!* If your child returns to the chair immediately you might say, "Good choice" or nothing at all. Otherwise, time-out for this event is over. Announce the negative consequence incurred and follow-through: "You didn't stay on the time-out chair. You can't play with Zoey today." Eventually, your child will see that going to the time-out chair and staying there is preferable to having no favorite toys, videos, snacks, or friends to play with all day.

"How Does Time-Out Work For Younger Children?"

For younger children the time-out description and steps followed are the same as for 6-to-8-year-olds. Explain time-out in terms young children can understand. The *shaping* technique can be used with younger children to teach time-out. Consider the following example:

Two-year-old Tyler frequently bites other children. Because of the serious nature of the behavior, his Mother has decided when that behavior occurs Tyler will immediately be placed in time-out (calmly and firmly). Further, all fun activities will be taken away for the next three hours (which is "forever" to a 2-year-old). These activities might include going to the park, having a friend come over, watching TV, enjoying preferred snacks, or playing with a favorite toy. The time-out explanation by Mom to Tyler is:

"Your friends are coming to play and visit with you today. Sometimes you get angry and bite Quincy and Sean. If you do that today, Mommy is going to tell them to go home and you are going to sit on this chair until this bell dings. (Demonstrate.) You are a little boy who knows self-control and you can learn to use your words or ask Mommy for help when you get upset. (Share your view of positive expectations of his behavior.) If Quincy won't give you this truck and you get angry and bite, Mommy is going to put you in the green chair and Quincy and Sean will go home. I'm going to help you remember today."

Stay in close proximity to your toddlers when they are around other young ones. Be especially vigilant of children 18-months-to-3-years-old. Hoping that things "go okay" can be dangerous. Staying close-by allows you to step in early and stop negative behaviors as or before they occur. Too, you can reinforce positive behaviors as they happen ("I like your sharing. That's nice."). Playtime for this group should be limited to one hour, under close supervision, so parents can intervene before their child bites or harms anyone. An alternative, appropriate behavior can be suggested: "Use your hands." Or, as child raises fist to hit, "Put your hands on your tummy." These social interactions are the learning ground for your toddlers in developing self-control.

"What About The Strong-Willed Child?"

Some children are very persistent or strong-willed by nature. They often do not give up easily and are more combative when it comes to discipline. Whenever possible, tailor discipline measures to your child's temperament or personality.

With the strong-willed child, help them save face and encourage them when you can. For example, you can say, "Great, you went to time-out; that wasn't easy." You might give the command to go to time-out, then turn your back and ignore them if they say, "No," watching instead for movement towards the chair. Then praise them once they move to comply. Try not to *rub it in* by continuing to reprimand them while they are in time-out. ("I don't know why you have to be so bullheaded! Why can't you just do what you are told?")

"When Do I Combine Charts With Time-Out?"

Parents often achieve desired changes using positive praise and attention alone, without having to resort to punishment. For example, by praising clear talk when it occurs, clear talk increases and whining decreases. With some children, point loss and time-out are not necessary. In other cases, negative behavior may not decrease enough, so that point loss and time-out are needed. If this is the case, proceed to Step 2 (below).

Step 1: Provide positive praise and attention only when the desired behavior occurs.

Step 2: Use a chart to provide positive points for desired

behavior and negative
points for the opposite behavior. Subtract the negative from the positive points
yielding a "Grand Total" of points which are then used to either earn or lose
privileges. (If the rate of negative behavior (whining, hitting) is still high following Steps 1 and 2, then implement Step 3.)
Step 3: Combine time-out with Step 2. Within a few days, if you are consistent,
negative behaviors will decrease and appropriate behaviors will increase.

Parents often say, "I feel as if I'm constantly taking things away. Do they have to 'earn' everything?" Keep in mind: **The purpose of ACP is to train parents to teach their child to follow predetermined rules.** If you are providing enough positive praise and attention to your child and are clear and consistent in expecting them to earn their privileges, this program will only last a few weeks. Your relationship with your child will change to one of them wanting to maintain the positive bond they are forming with you; to want to continue to please you. You may have already noticed that they are behaving more positively and wanting to please you more.

Though parents are often reluctant to make their children *suffer*, training children to respect parental authority is essential to healthy child development. Children must be taught to obey home rules. And, doing many of the things they enjoy (playing, watching TV, having friends over, etc.) should occur only when they consistently follow rules such as:

• Coming when called
• Talking respectfully
• Completing daily chores

KIDS *ALL WOUND-UP* AND YOU'RE *ALL WOUND DOWN?*

How to Eliminate Struggle-Time at Bedtime

You've had a long day and you're looking forward to some free time after you put your young kids to bed. Unfortunately, by the time they've heard just one more story, had one more cup of water, and one more kiss and hug, your nerves are frazzled, your free time is spent, and you find yourself feeling increasingly frustrated and angry. Your tolerance level is exceeded and you yell, "Get in bed and stay there!"

What you had intended to be a special time of warmth and closeness has ended in a battle, with parent and children feeling angry, upset, and negative toward each other. For many parents, the battle does not end once their children are asleep. Children often awake in the middle of the night and the cycle continues or new problems arise.

Young children may dread and resist bedtime for many reasons: A fear of darkness, fear they may be harmed, not wanting to separate from parents and give up their attention, or simply not wanting to stop a fun activity. Sleep requires a *letting go* of current awareness, and succumbing to an unconscious state. This process can be frightening to many children. Encouraging your child to share her bedtime concerns will pave the way for a smoother "good night" experience.

Maintaining control at your child's bedtime requires that you understand how you may be reinforcing the problems you want to eliminate. Yelling at your child, "You never listen to me! Why can't you just go to bed and stay there?" is a form of negative attention (a type of reinforcement) which actually serves to increase the negative behavior (getting out of bed). Your goal is to increase the times your child stays in bed at bedtime.

Parents often do not give firm, clear commands to their children at bedtime. Instead, they use "question" commands ("How about going to bed now?") or "let's" commands ("Let's get ready for bed now.") which sets the child up for non-compliance. Children are much more responsive to brief, direct, and firm commands telling them exactly what you expect them to do.

Relaxation and anger control training are an essential and often overlooked part of the bedtime regimen. Have the skills well rehearsed before you attempt to change the bedtime routine.

If Your Child Won't Go To Bed:

Establish a bedtime and stick to it. Children feel more secure and learn more quickly with consistency. They handle matters better when they are prepared. Establish a simple bedtime routine. For younger children, this can be brushing teeth and reading a bedtime story. For older children, you may want to set aside this time to talk about their day. Keep the routine calm and quiet. It is important to choose an activity that you feel you can carry out. For example, if you are too tired to read stories and you become frustrated and irritable while reading, then do something you like more (singing a song, saying a prayer, etc.).

Give your child a blessing. Regardless of the type of day you or your child had, it is nice to end it by giving them some form of blessing. You might express gratitude that they belong to you, that you appreciate their uniqueness and that they have a great destiny ahead which is theirs alone. One blessing we gave our kids was: *May God bless you and keep you. May He shine His face upon you and protect you wherever you go. May you feel His and my love deep in your heart.* They loved it! (And we said it and meant it, even when we weren't feeling too positive about how they had behaved that day!)

Use positive reinforcement to encourage good behavior. This can be as simple as praising your child when he goes to bed on time, or working out a reward system for consecutive nights of no bedtime struggles.

If Your Child Won't Stay In Bed

Use positive reinforcement and loss of privileges. If your child stays in bed, reward her the following day with points toward an activity or privilege she enjoys. If she continues to get up every few minutes, establish a set punishment, such as an earlier bedtime the next night or privilege loss the next day. (For example: Every time she gets out of bed, she loses ½ hour of playtime, ½ hour of TV time, etc.)

For children who are just learning to talk, try systematic ignoring for up to 20 minutes at a time. If your child starts to cry, and you have no reason to believe that she is in pain, let her cry. Wait at least five, but no more than 20, minutes and then go back into her room. Be gentle, but firm: Tell her that it is time to go to sleep now, give her a good night kiss, and leave the room. If you stick to this routine, she will soon realize that her tactics no longer work. However, if you spend a lot of time cuddling and soothing her, you can expect a repeat performance tomorrow night and every night.

If Your Young Child Wants To Sleep In Your Bed With You

Prevention is key: Do not allow your child to sleep in your bed. If they are ill, use an intercom, or sleep in the room with them. Though there are opposing opinions, many psychologists believe that it may be unhealthy for a child to sleep with parents on a regular basis. Research shows that children who regularly sleep with their parents tend to be less compliant in general. In addition to becoming overly dependent, the child may experience confusion about their role in the family, about their parents' relationship, or their own sexual feelings. If you wake up and find your child in your bed, do not allow them to stay there. Take your child back to their bed.

You might consider the following:

Block the doorway to your room, or hang a bell on the door. If they know you can hear them coming, they are less likely to try sneaking into bed with you.

Use rewards to reinforce positive behaviors and mild punishments as consequences for unwanted behaviors.

Establish ground rules regarding bedtime behavior and enforce them. If your children know and understand the rules, they are more likely to comply. If your response to their behavior is consistent and predictable, they will be less likely to try to manipulate you. Also, they will suffer less confusion about what is acceptable and what is unacceptable. Ultimately, your child's behavior is dependent upon the consequences you provide and the consistency with which you implement them.

It may help to pose these questions:
1. "After being put to bed, why does my child keep getting out of bed and calling for me?"
2. "What am I doing to reinforce that behavior?"
3. "What do I need to do to turn the situation around and teach them that they must go to bed, that they must stay there, and that they cannot sleep with me?"

Children respond well to loving words and praise. Incorporate positive reinforcement into your bedtime

strategies whenever possible and you will have more peaceful nights. And, you will maintain a positive relationship with your child.

"IF AT FIRST YOU DON'T SUCCEED . . ."

After You've Tried and Tried Again

Some days it may appear as if every link in your daily chain of events is the weakest link. Your child may wake up cranky, contrary, and defiant, and *nothing you try works*. Perhaps they went to bed too late, are sick, or just out of sorts. In that instance, put discipline aside. Instead, hold and nurture your child before making demands or trying to engage them in daily routine expectations (to get dressed, eat). If you impose the usual discipline regimen for whining, complaining, and not obeying, the situation may deteriorate.

While consistency is critical, you also need to keep in mind that you don't need to win every battle to win the war. Sometimes it's best to just let things go for that event, sit down and figure out what transpired, learn from it, and be prepared for the next time a similar situation arises. A new opportunity to implement the ACP tools is probably hours away! If, after being told "No," your teen screams at you and storms away angrily, you don't need to chase after him to make things right *now!* Just mark down any points/privileges he lost during the interchange and enforce them. He will learn that you still followed through with consequences for his behavior.

If your young child is having a day where their irritability level is ricocheting off mountain tops, for whatever reason, you should be flexible. Hold them and help them do the things they are normally expected to do independently. Firmly tell them the sequence of events. When you are clear and predictable they will more likely follow your lead:

After rocking a cranky five-year-old Ryan Michelle for 5-to-10 minutes, Mom says, "Ryan Michelle, I'm going to help you get ready this morning. First we'll get dressed, eat, brush your teeth, and then I'll put on a music CD for you to listen to until it's time to leave for school."

Do not confuse the whiny protest that often occurs in response to commands with being out of sorts. But, once in a while, it is reasonable to expect your child to have an *off* day. When that occurs, guide them through the routine with as little conflict and frustration as possible. Look for positives and praise them. Maybe you'll be lucky and their mood will turn around.

We can't control everything!

REFERENCES

Becker, W.C. *Parents Are Teachers*. Champaign, Ill.: Research Press, 1971.

Forehand, R. L. & McMahon, R. J. *Helping the Noncompliant Child: A clinician's guide to parent training*. New York: Guilford Press, 1981.

Hanf, C. & Kling, J. *Facilitating Parent-Child Interaction: A two-stage training model*. Unpublished Manuscript, University of Oregon Medical School, 1973.

Luthar, S. S. (2003). *The* culture of affluence: Psychological costs of material wealth. *Child Development*, 74, 1581-1593.

Novaco, R. W. (1977). A Stress Inoculation Approach to Anger Management in Training of Law Enforcement Officers. *American Journal of Community Psychology*, 5, 327-346.

Patterson, G. R. *Living with Children*. (Rev ed.) Champaign, Ill.: Research Press, 1976.

Patterson, G.R. *Families: Applications of social learning to family life*. (Rev.ed). Champaign, Ill.: Research Press, 1975.

Patterson, G.R. *The aggressive child: Victim and architect of a coercive system*. In E.J. Mash, L.A. Hamerlynck, & L.C. Handy (Eds.), Behavior modification and families. New York: Brunner/Mazel, 1976.

Sudjian, S. & Lamphear, V. L. *Evaluation of an Anger Control Parenting Program*. Unpublished Manuscript, 1995.

Wallerstein, J. S., Lewis, J. M., & Blakeslee, S. *The Unexpected Legacy of Divorce*. New York: Hyperion, 2000.